Jennifer Day

thread stories

A VISUAL GUIDE TO CREATING STUNNING STITCHED PORTRAIT QUILTS

C&T PUBLISHING

Text and photography copyright © 2015 by Jennifer Day

Publisher: Amy Marson

Creative Director: Gailen Runge

Art Director: Kristy Zacharias

Editor: Lynn Koolish

Technical Editor: Helen Frost

Cover Designers: Christina Jarumay Fox and Kristy Zacharias

Book Designer: Christina Jarumay Fox

Production Coordinator: Freesia Pearson Blizard

Production Editor: Joanna Burgarino

Photography by Jennifer Day, unless otherwise noted

Photography on pages 91–100 by the individual artists, unless otherwise noted

Published by C&T Publishing, Inc., P.O. Box 1456, Lafayette, CA 94549

Library of Congress Cataloging-in-Publication Data

Day, Jennifer, 1955-

Thread stories : a visual guide to creating stunning stitched portrait quilts / Jennifer Day.

pages cm

ISBN 978-1-61745-053-2 (soft cover)

1. Quilting. 2. Art quilts. 3. Portraits on quilts. 4. Photographs on cloth. 5. Fabric pictures. I. Title.

TT835.D386 2015

746.46--dc23

2015008956

Printed in China

10 9 8 7 6 5 4 3 2 1

contents

Introduction: Quilts Are Stories...5

Photographs That Tell a Story...7

Elements of a Great Photo ▪ *Editing the Photo*

Tools and Supplies...9

Sewing Machine ▪ *Sewing Machine Needles* ▪ *Free-Motion Presser Foot* ▪ *Printable Paper-Backed Fabric* ▪ *Canvas* ▪ *Batting* ▪ *Scissors and Thread Snips* ▪ *Ruler* ▪ *Backing and Binding Fabric*

Threads!...13

Gütermann Thread ▪ *Presencia Thread* ▪ *Isacord Embroidery Thread* ▪ *Silk Thread* ▪ *Variegated Thread*

Photographs and Cameras...17

Environmental Portraits ▪ *Cropping* ▪ *Digital Cameras and Image Size* ▪ *Pixels, Megapixels, Resolution, PPI, and DPI* ▪ *Copyright*

Using Photo-Editing Software...23

Make Your Photo the Best It Can Be ▪ *Posterization* ▪ *More Posterization Examples*

Printing on Fabric...32

Types of Fabric ▪ *Sizes of Fabric* ▪ *Poster Printing*

Getting Started...34

Making a Quilt Sandwich ▪ *Blending Is Key* ▪ *Stitching Direction*

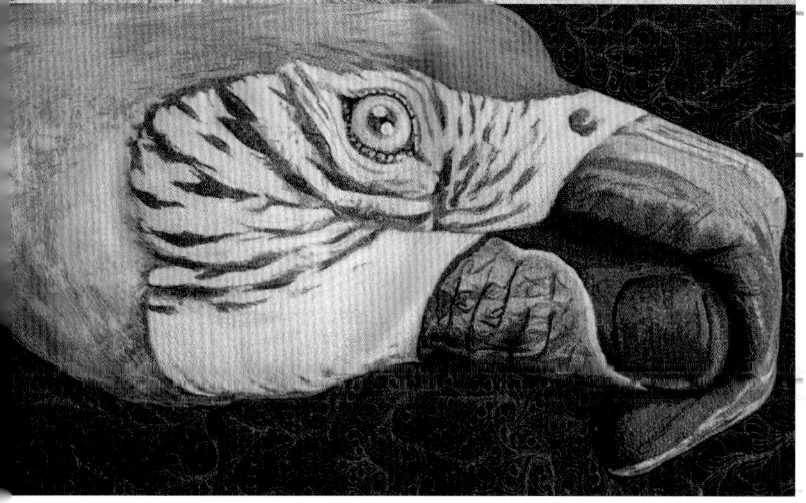

THE EYES HAVE IT ... 40

- *The Irises* ▪ *The Whites*
- *Stitching the Eyes* ▪ *Highlights*
- *Eyelashes*

BLENDING SKIN TONES ... 48

- *Auditioning Threads*
- *Starting the Blending Process*
- *Elisha (Diverse Skin Tones)*
- *Judy (Elderly Skin)* ▪ *Texture* ▪ *Lips*
- *Eyes* ▪ *Carson (Youthful Skin)*

HAIR ... 59

- *Dark Hair* ▪ *Streaks of Light*
- *White and Gray Hair* ▪ *Blonds*

HANDS ... 65

- *Elderly Hands* ▪ *Young Hands*

CLOTHING ... 69

- *Using Free-Motion Quilting*
- *Completely Covering in Thread*
- *Appliqué* ▪ *Combination*

PET PORTRAITS ... 73

- *Taking the Perfect Pet Portrait* ▪ *Eyes*
- *Mouth* ▪ *Fur* ▪ *Whiskers* ▪ *Birds*

Free-Motion Quilting ... 81

- *Choosing a Free-Motion Design*

Correcting Mistakes ... 85

- *Don't Be Too Hard on Yourself*
- *Using Appliqué* ▪ *Cutting to Remove Bubbles*
- *Covering Over White Dots*

On the Flip Side ... 89

Guest Fiber Artists ... 91

- *Barbara McKie* ▪ *Jayne Bentley Gaskins*
- *Lea McComas* ▪ *Susan Brubaker Knapp*

Student Work ... 95

Jennifer Day Portrait Quilts ... 101

About the Author/Resources ... 111

introduction: quilts are stories

Quilts are wonderful stories. In days gone by, a quilt was lovingly created by a mother, grandmother, or friend who wanted to tell a story in fabric. The tale could have been utilitarian in its roots or it could have been a labor of love. Either way, the creator spent many hours working with a needle making the quilt.

The creator's heart and soul went into the quilt's seams. Whether the quilt was only a patchwork square used to cover a mattress that was supported by ropes threaded through the bed frame in a home with no running water, or a quilt for the firstborn child in the family, the artist told a story.

Storytelling through quiltmaking has been a common theme throughout the ages. Quilters have illustrated the births of children, marriages, slavery, civil rights, suffrage, teaching, friendship, and death.

Let There Be Light, which hung at the United Nations in Geneva, Switzerland, in 2013, is the story of a woman in Africa holding a solar lantern provided by Solar Sisters, a humanitarian organization devoted to bringing electricity to parts of the world that have none. The story of this woman, seen with her husband and child bathed in light, is a story worth sharing.

Siempre Esperanza, which hung at the United Nations in Geneva, Switzerland, in 2011, is a quilt that speaks to issues of peace and conflict that women must face all over the world. This woman is from Oaxaca, Mexico. Her life is tangled in the world of drug cartels. Her stories are unimaginable. This quilt shared its story with thousands of people while it hung at the United Nations.

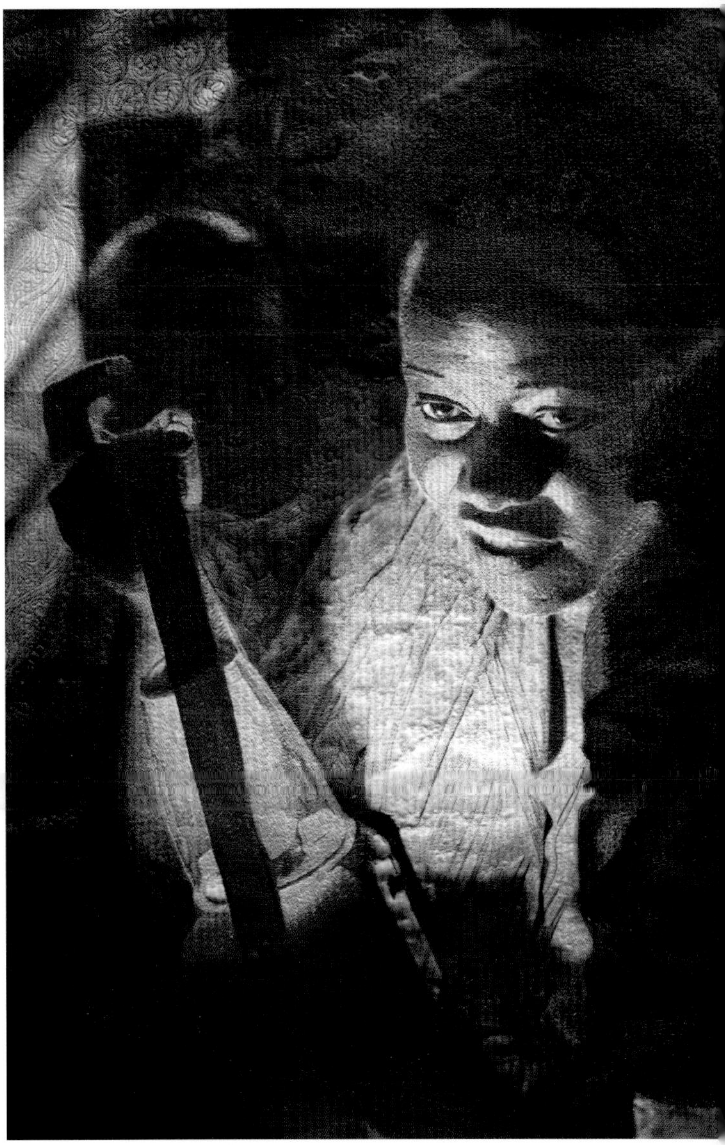

Let There Be Light by Jennifer Day, 24″ × 30″, 2013

Siempre Esperanza by Jennifer Day, 24″ × 30″, 2011

The Thread Stories technique starts with a photograph printed on fabric that is then covered in thread, creating art based on realism. This technique can be used on any photograph—from landscapes and nature scenes, to portraits of loved ones and pets, to human-interest images. The process is the same. Some refer to this technique as thread painting.

Working primarily with portraiture in this book, we'll explore choosing a photograph and learning how to prepare and print the photo on fabric. We'll also work through the process of stitching. You will learn how to select threads and how to apply them to achieve a realistic portrait, enhancing the art with deep hues or soft tones. To finish up, we'll look at how free-motion quilting completes the work.

Come join me on the journey into Thread Stories.

photographs that tell a story

The most important component to making a Thread Stories quilt is choosing the right photograph. If you have a smartphone, you probably always have a camera with you. Photos taken on the street, at a party, in your backyard, or in a crowded train station—these are what I call *environmental* photographs and are the best ones to use in telling a story. Capturing a moment is the mission of an environmental photograph.

The photograph at right of a man taking an afternoon snooze in a doorway on the streets of Santa Fe, New Mexico, on a cold winter day is a perfect example. I took this photograph with the camera I had at hand—my iPhone. There is an instant story being told here—I was curious because it was a cold day, but the man's jacket was bundled behind his head and his belly was exposed to the elements. What is he holding in his hands under his shirt? Why did he choose to take a nap on a crowded street in Santa Fe? Why has he chosen to wear a bandana around his head? Is he an old hippie with a story to tell, or is he something else altogether?

The photo also has a fabulous backdrop—a building that dates back to the 1600s, with its cracked plaster and architectural detail. The aqua door has good color balance with the rose plaster and complements the texture of the old brick.

Elements of a Great Photo Background

One of the most important elements of a good photograph is the background. Always be aware of how the background will add dimension and interest to the shot. Keep in mind that the subject does not need to be centered if there is something that adds to the story to the left or the right.

What's the Story?

Before you lift your camera to shoot, ask yourself the following questions:

- What do I want to say?
- What emotions am I trying to capture?
- What is my ultimate message?

Asking yourself questions such as these makes it easier to know how to approach the subject of the photograph.

Get Close

Every face has the potential to tell a unique story and the power to reveal a person's past or uncover an individual's deepest emotions. While shooting a portrait, getting closer to the individual allows for an intimate view. A Thread Stories portrait quilt needs a close-up photograph so that the details in the face can be shown well in thread.

Find the Best Angle

As you move toward your subject, move to each side as you view the image in your camera. Your goal is to select the angle that best captures the subject and the background in the photograph. You may take ten or more pictures of a person from many different angles to get the one that you will use in your quilt.

TIP

With digital cameras, it's easy to take a lot of pictures so you can capture just what you are looking for.

Lighting

How does light affect your story? Is the light interesting or is it flat and lifeless? You may need to move around the subject to get the light to fall correctly on the individual's face.

EDITING THE PHOTO

After you have selected your photo, decide whether or not it needs editing. Editing can be done in Adobe Photoshop, Adobe Photoshop Elements, or in any number of other photo-editing programs. Basic programs (and even smartphone apps) allow you to crop and adjust the exposure, clarity, contrast, or saturation of a photo.

note

In this book, I will be using Photoshop Elements in the examples, but most photo-editing software works in a similar manner.

The photo below has all the elements of a great photo. The emotions are quickly identified—compassion, sadness, and curiosity. The child's dirty face and her expression cause you to wonder about her life. The barbed wire twisted around the wooden stays and the rusted metal building behind her adds another layer to the photo and the story. She lives in the dump in Chinandega, Nicaragua, in a house made of boards and tin. A photograph such as this will make a wonderful quilt because it sends a strong message and tells a thought-provoking, emotional story.

tools and supplies

After you have selected your photograph, you will not need many supplies for the techniques presented in this book. The following are the basics (each is described in detail in this chapter):

- Sewing machine
- Sturdy needle for thread painting and free-motion embroidery
- Free-motion presser foot
- Printable paper-backed fabric
- Canvas
- Batting
- Backing and binding fabric
- Scissors and thread snips
- Ruler

SEWING MACHINE

Any sewing machine, even your grandmother's, will work for this technique. The needle just needs to move up and down, and you need to be able to drop the feed dogs.

The Brother Nouvelle 1500SI is a good basic domestic machine. It is a workhorse that has just a straight stitch and a dial on the front of the machine to lower the feed dogs.

I also use a Handi Quilter Sweet Sixteen sit-down machine for my larger quilts. If you love to free-motion quilt but struggle to fit your project in the small throat space of a domestic sewing machine, you'll love the HQ Sweet Sixteen. It has 16″ of throat space, which gives you room to quilt artworks that are as large as a king-size quilt. With the large throat space, you can roll the fabric close to the motor and move the fabric to either side without restrictions. My largest quilt measured 72″ × 72″. The Sweet Sixteen was a lifesaver on that project. It comes with a table that gives you room to work, and it has a powerful motor that quilts with ease and stitches up to 1,500 stitches per minute.

Sewing Machine Needles

I normally use size 14 needles. Janome now has begun manufacturing a pink-tip needle for free-motion quilting that can be used in this thread-painting process. You may be more comfortable using a stronger needle that will not cause needle deflection (page 88). Try using a size 16 or 18 needle.

Free-Motion Presser Foot

A special foot is needed for free-motion work. The foot is called a free-motion foot or darning foot and is typically sold with the machine.

I frequently will sew at 1,000–1,300 stitches per minute. This fast pace makes the open-toe style essential to success. If your machine did not come with an open-toe foot, you can buy one from your sewing machine manufacturer or your local quilt shop. You will need to verify the length of the shaft before purchasing a universal foot.

TIP

If your free-motion foot isn't open-toe, it's easy to simply cut an opening at the front of either a metal or plastic foot with a hacksaw and file down any rough edges.

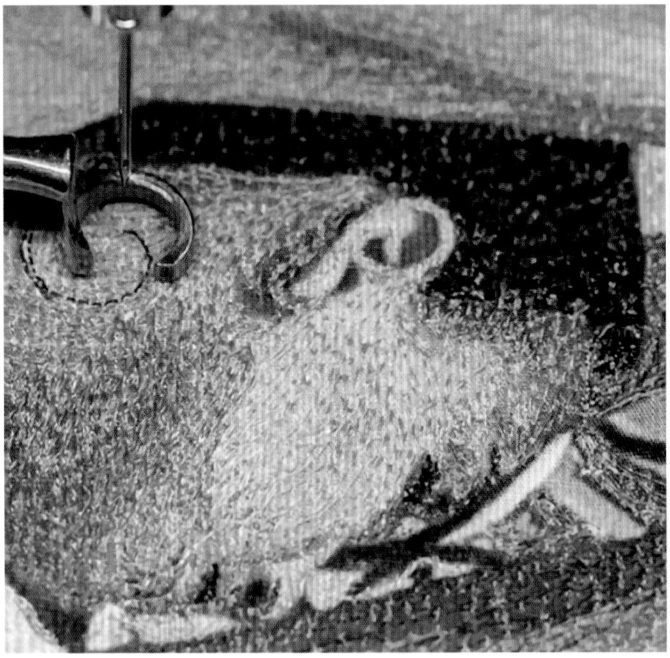

PRINTABLE PAPER-BACKED FABRIC

Refer to Printing on Fabric (page 32).

CANVAS

It is important to stabilize your artwork as you begin the thread-painting process. I use canvas to stabilize the photo fabric, as it will be intensely covered in thread. A #10 (15-ounce) unprimed, natural heavyweight 100% cotton artist canvas works well. Big Duck, a 15-ounce canvas, is readily available online by the yard or in rolls (see Resources, page 111).

If you use a 10-ounce canvas, it will buckle and stretch as you add more thread to the stitched surface. This may be the look you want if the image has clothing with movement (as in the dress in *Abuela*, below and at right) or if you want to add additional texture to a portion of the image.

Details from *Abuela* (see full quilt, page 101)

BATTING

There are many different types of batting available on the market. For a quilt stitched with this technique you can use any batting you like.

If you use a fabric with a photo printed on it, canvas, and backing cloth, you have met the industry definition of a quilt. Batting is only necessary if you choose to use a binding that is finished by hand. Hand stitching the binding and catching the layer next to the backing cloth is very difficult if that layer is canvas. The use of batting as the layer between the canvas and backing cloth makes it much easier to stitch by hand.

SCISSORS AND THREAD SNIPS

Thread snips allow you to snip your threads quickly and easily. My technique is all about thread, and the Thrifty Clips snips are perfect. They are 4½″ long and easily fit in my hand. I will typically have two pairs sitting nearby at all times. I always pull my bobbin threads to the top of the fabric with every change of thread or when moving the needle to another spot. I may snip as many as 40 threads in an hour of sewing. The right snips are critical to my ability to sew for hours at a time.

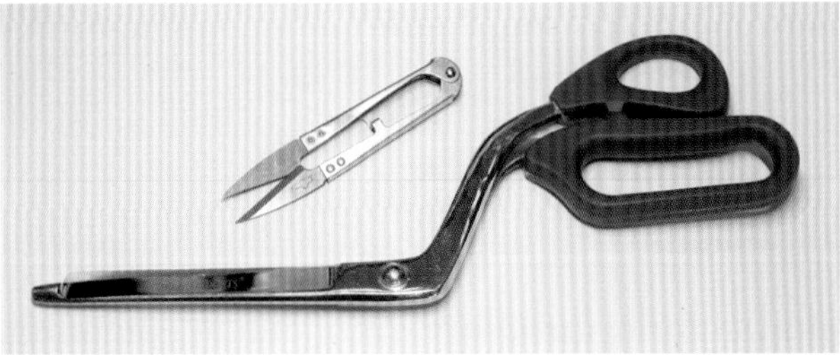

Thrifty Clips available from WAWAK (see Resources, page 111)

When you cut canvas, a sturdy pair of scissors is essential. Scissors designed for cutting batting are perfect. I use a pair from Handi Quilter that has a long blade that sits flat on the table or counter. It is a wonderful tool for cutting canvas as well as batting (see Resources, page 111).

note

I don't use a rotary cutter or a mat for cutting my fabrics and canvas. I leave approximately 4″ around all the edges of my quilt. When I'm done stitching, I use sharp scissors to cut the final shape of the quilt.

RULER

When you have finished all the stitching, use a straightedge to square the quilt by drawing lines on the fabric with a fine-tip black marker. There are many ruler or straightedge options available.

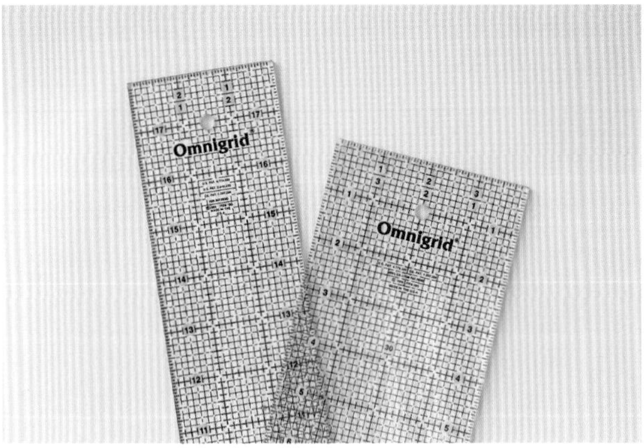

BACKING AND BINDING FABRIC

You can use any fabric you like for the backing and binding of your quilt. I prefer to use the same fabric for both. I use a fabric with very small print or no print. A nice muted batik is a good choice. A solid color works best with a white or cream bobbin. This will give the quilt a ghostlike appearance on the reverse side (see On the Flip Side, page 89).

threads!

The Thread Stories technique is the process of thread painting—using the needle as a paintbrush to paint with thread over a photograph on fabric to create a realistic image. Mine is a renegade approach to thread painting—from a distance people perceive my art as a painting. Only when they get closer do they see the individual threads and understand that the artwork is sewn. When they step back again, they see a portrait.

Thread painting refers to dense machine stitching, using different colors of thread in close proximity to create realistic images. Soft values of the same color create shadows and highlights, bringing the portrait to life.

Thread is the most essential component of the Thread Stories technique. The quilt top is your canvas and the thread is your paint. I have accumulated almost 2,000 different threads in my "paint box" at my disposal in my studio. The reason I have so many threads is that I need the minute gradations of color and value between colors. A full paint box is integral to the success of my portraiture.

> **TIP**
>
> Your thread stash will grow as you make more quilts using this technique. You won't know what colors you need until you start planning each quilt. As you create more art, your collection of threads will grow.

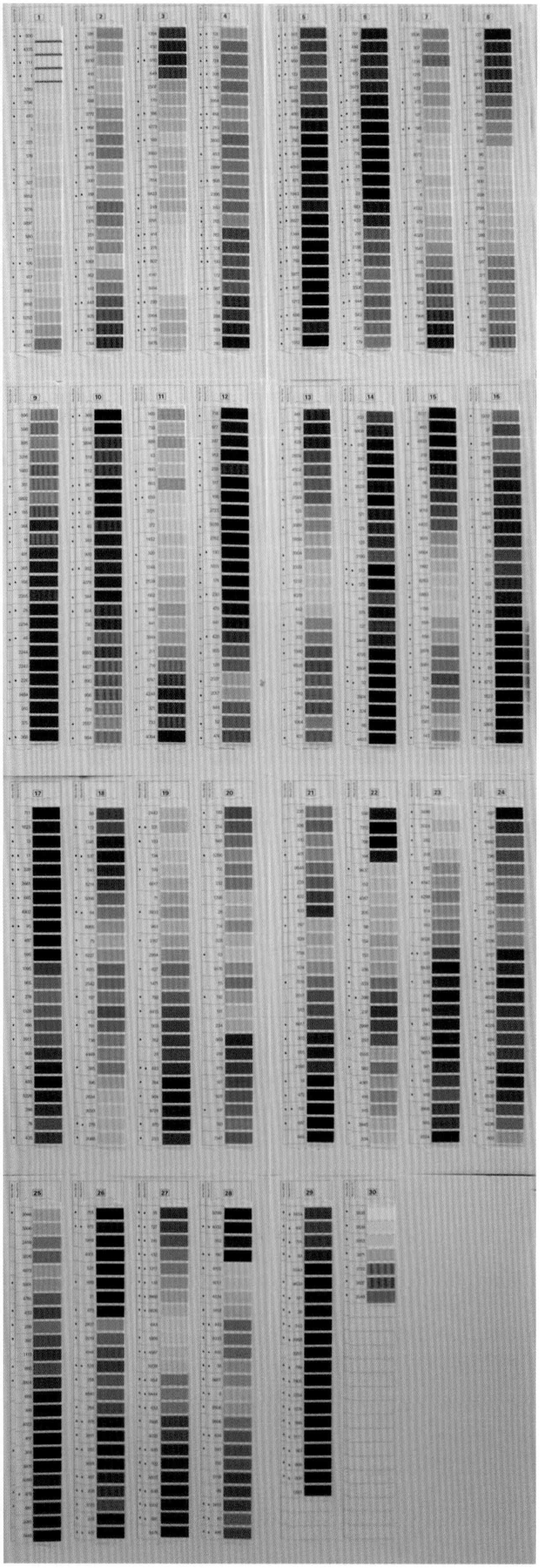

GÜTERMANN THREAD

My thread line of choice is by Gütermann. I use Mara 100 and Mara 70. Mara 100 is a 30-weight thread and Mara 70 is a 40-weight thread. The Mara line of polyester threads was developed for the garment industry. It is a matte thread with no luster. (You can imagine the number of different colors of threads needed to create garments. Each thread needs to match the color of the cloth exactly.) This precise coloration is essential to the success of a Thread Stories quilt. Unfortunately, this thread is not available in local quilt stores. It is available online in 1,000 m and 5,000 m spools (see Resources, page 111).

There are currently 692 colors available in the Mara 70 line. I use all 692 colors in my quilts. The minute gradations of Gütermann threads are critical to the success of my quilting technique.

PRESENCIA THREAD

I also use a line of threads from Presencia that is readily available in quilt shops. It is a 100% cotton, matte, no-luster three-ply thread. There are currently 180 colors of thread in the Presencia line.

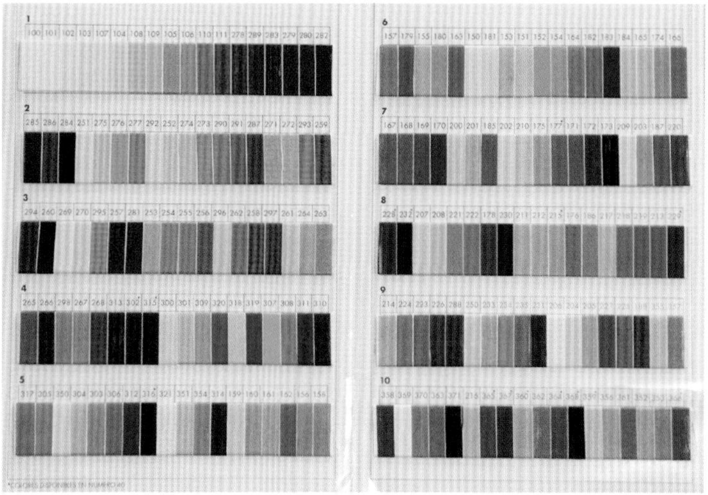

ISACORD EMBROIDERY THREAD

When you need just a dash of brightness and shine, embroidery threads can be the perfect choice. Isacord currently has 351 colors in its embroidery thread line.

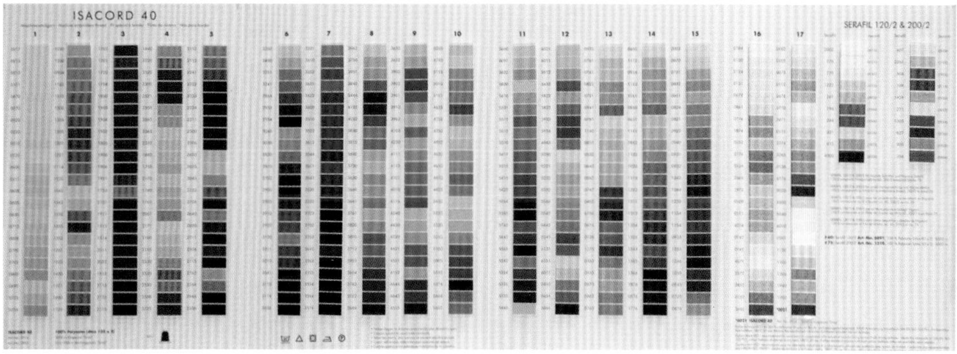

SILK THREAD

Use silk threads for the same purpose as embroidery threads—when you need a thread that catches light, the reflective quality of the silk can add luminosity. Silk is available in many thread weights. The key is selecting the right weight of thread for the application. If the goal is to cover an area in silk thread, a 30-weight thread is best. The sheen of the silk is more apparent when the threads are laid closely together. There is no reason to use 100-weight when thread painting—the thread is too thin and recedes into the cloth, making it useless at bringing attention to the area being stitched.

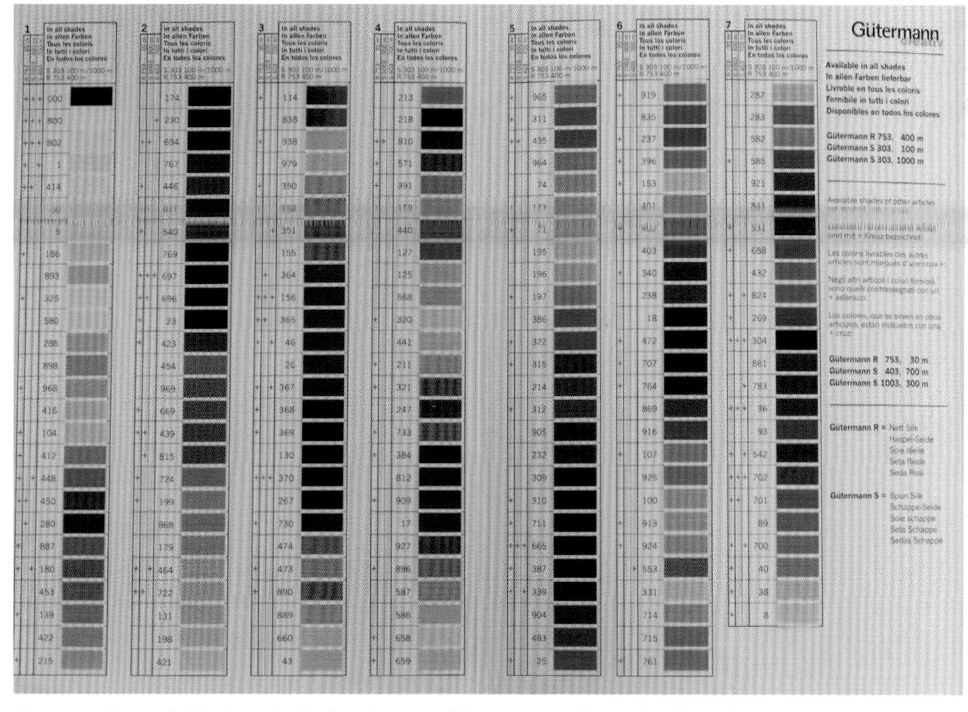

Many vendors sell silk threads. My favorites are Gütermann and Superior Threads.

Detail from *It's Raining Cats and Dogs* (see full quilt, page 73)

The whiskers of this cat are 30-weight silk thread.

VARIEGATED THREAD

Because variegated threads change colors along the strands of thread, I do not recommend using them for this style of thread painting. The variation of colors can be random, and you lose control over how the colors are placed on your quilt.

Do consider using variegated threads for free-motion quilting in the background of the quilt. They can add interest to a blank canvas if the background is a solid color.

TIP

It's a good idea to buy thread color cards so you can see what threads are available from each manufacturer. This is especially helpful if you need to buy thread online (see Resources, page 111).

photographs and cameras

Choosing a photograph is the most critical part of the Thread Stories process. Each photograph that you consider should contain a story that is easily interpreted by the viewer. Your photos are winners if they elicit emotion.

ENVIRONMENTAL PORTRAITS

An *environmental portrait* is a photograph of a person taken in his or her normal setting, or environment. This can be in the individual's home or workplace, on the street, in a park, at a carnival—you get the idea. By photographing a person in his or her natural surroundings, you can more easily identify the individual's character and therefore portray the essence of that person's personality.

Thread Stories portraits are based on photographs that are rich in detail. Close-up images always work best for this technique. Because of the width and texture of the thread, a subject that is very small and far away will lose detail and will become unreadable to the eye after it is covered in thread. Your portrait should be easily readable to the viewer.

CROPPING

After you have selected a photograph for your project, you may want to crop the image so that details of the subject are seen in more detail and distracting elements are removed.

At right are images of a beautiful young girl in a shopping cart in a grocery store. She was perched in the cart, eating a banana, with flowers behind her as her grandmother pushed the cart. I was never sure whether she was given the banana because she was misbehaving and this was the perfect way to distract her, or whether she got the banana as a reward for being a perfect child. The story is one of simple joy.

I chose to crop the photograph so as to focus on the girl's face, allowing the bits of banana to be easily seen on her lips.

Another environmental photograph shows a young girl running through a crowd, clutching a Tootsie Pop and her stuffed animal. I was in Nicaragua that day, visiting the inhabited dump in Chinandega. The photograph of this little girl tells the story of the families who live in the dump with little sanitation. Her dirty face and hands clutching her treasures tell a story. Again, I cropped the photograph to allow more detail in the photograph to be painted with thread. By leaving the Tootsie Pop and her buddy in the photo, I was still able to tell the story.

There is a lot going on in the photo below. By cropping, I narrowed the focus to the two-year-old child wandering the beach unattended and the herd of cattle tended by a young boy on horseback. Further cropping focuses all the viewer's attention on the young boy and his dogs. He has had fun playing in the mud. It looks like a swim in the ocean is in store for him to clean him up!

If you capture your subject with close-up photography, look for clarity in the photograph. The more detail in the picture, the more detail you will have to work with in your art.

DIGITAL CAMERAS AND IMAGE SIZE

The most common types of digital cameras today are smartphone cameras, point-and-shoot cameras, and digital single-lens reflex (DSLR) cameras. The quality of the photos and the megapixel capacity of these cameras are based on many factors, but for our purposes, what you need really depends on how big you want to print your images.

As of the writing of this book, inexpensive point-and-shoot cameras have upward of 16 megapixels, the newest cell phone cameras are commonly in the 8–16 megapixel range, and any DSLR should provide plenty of megapixels. Most reasonably new digital cameras (including cell phone cameras) will be just fine to get you started with the Thread Stories technique.

PIXELS, MEGAPIXELS, RESOLUTION, PPI, AND DPI

A *pixel* is essentially a dot of color stored either in your camera or on the computer. A *megapixel* (*MP*) is one million pixels. The more pixels in an image (measured in *pixels per inch*, or *ppi*), the clearer (or bigger) the image is when you look at it on your computer and the bigger you can print it.

Resolution determines the quality of the image and is measured in ppi (pixels per inch) for digital images and *dpi* (*dots per inch*) for printed images. The higher the resolution, the better your image will look. The more megapixels an image has when you shoot it, the higher the ppi and dpi can be when you view or print the image, resulting in a clearer, sharper, and larger picture.

I like to print my images at 300 ppi/dpi (see Pixels, Megapixels, Resolution, PPI, and DPI, page 19). At this resolution, without any image-editing manipulation (see Using Photo-Editing Software, page 23), a 10 MP image is about 9″ × 12″ and a 20 MP image is about 13″ × 16″—the more megapixels, the bigger the image.

Smaller photos can be enlarged so you can make a bigger quilt. The bigger image may not be as sharp, and you may lose some detail, but as you stitch over the photograph you can decide at that time how best to proceed.

The photo below is a close-up image of an 85-year-old woman, Marcelena, in the Dominican Republic. My son and I were working with locals, tearing down and rebuilding the cardboard and tin shack building that she had called home for the last 40 years. In this photo, taken with an 18 MP camera, you can easily see the pores and wrinkles on her face; you can even see the cataracts in her eyes. When creating my quilts, I look for this level of detail in my photographs because I want to capture every nuance. For me, this is what is necessary to create realism in this art form.

Taken with an 18-megapixel camera

The photo below was taken with an 8 MP iPhone camera. Notice that the lines of the woman's face are softer. The photo was printed at the same size as the previous one, but because there are fewer pixels to work with it has a lower resolution and less detail. You can still create a fabulous portrait quilt using this photo, but you'll need to work a bit harder to create the details in your final work of art.

Taken with an 8-megapixel camera

The picture of my son and the woman was also taken with an iPhone and is a bit blurry because the camera moved while I was taking the photo. A photo such as this is certainly usable for a Thread Stories quilt, but you will have to use your imagination to fill in the details such as the distinctive wrinkles in the woman's face.

Taken with an 8-megapixel camera, but the camera moved when I was taking the shot

COPYRIGHT

If you are using your own photograph for your art quilt there are no copyright issues. However, if you have found a photograph online or elsewhere that you want to use in your art, you **must** get written permission from the photographer (or whoever holds the copyright) **and** you may need to pay for the rights to use the photograph. A professional photographer, Jason Tozer, took the below photograph of a dancer. I contacted Jason, asked for permission to use his photograph, and paid him $200 for the rights.

When you ask for permission and purchase rights, it is important to understand exactly what you have permission to do with the photograph and how the photographer wishes to be credited. For example, I used Jason's photograph and added butterflies using Photoshop. It is also important to give credit when you are showing the work or if it is published. I give credit to Jason as the photographer on the back of the quilt and when entering quilt shows.

Photo by Jason Tozer

Butterflies Are Free by Jennifer Day, based on a photograph by Jason Tozer, 35″ × 52″, 2014

I purchased the photo at right from Barbara Grover for $200. I was unable to travel to Darfur to photograph solar cooking for my quilt *Cooking with the Sun*. Obtaining her permission to use her photography was a perfect solution to my travel issues.

There are many stock photography sites online that sell photographs. Be sure to read the usage agreements to see what you are and aren't allowed to do with the purchased photos.

Photo by Barbara Grover

Detail from *Cooking with the Sun* (see full quilt, page 106)

using photo-editing software

note

The examples in this chapter were created using Adobe Photoshop Elements version 12. If you have a different version, the functionality will be the same but the screen layouts may be a bit different and you may need to use slightly different paths. The results will be the same.

BEFORE YOU BEGIN

To keep your original photo safe, it's best to save the photo with a new name before you start working with it. From the menu bar, click on *File*; then select *Save As* from the drop-down menu and enter a new file name.

There is an abundance of photo-editing software on today's market. The most popular is Adobe Photoshop. Adobe sells a smaller, less expensive version of Photoshop—Photoshop Elements. Photoshop Elements is affordable and will do everything necessary to adjust your photos for use in your quilting. Some of the functions that are important to take advantage of are layers, posterization, exposure, contrast, highlights and shadows, clarity, sharpening, and saturation. There are many books and online tutorials available that can teach you how to use Photoshop and Photoshop Elements. I encourage you to purchase one or look online and begin to experiment.

MAKE YOUR PHOTO THE BEST IT CAN BE

The first step in preparing a photo is to use your photo-editing software to make the photo as good as it can be. This can include adjusting the color, shadows and highlights, brightness and contrast, and vibrancy, and sharpening it. When printing on fabric it's also a good idea to increase the saturation anywhere from 10 to 25 percent because fabric is more absorbent than paper. Many times I will adjust the contrast and clarity as well. When you have the photo just the way you want it, save it.

CLEAN UP PHOTOS WITH THE CLONE STAMP TOOL

While this book doesn't cover the many things you can do to a photograph, I do want to mention one tool that I often use. It's called the *Clone Stamp Tool*. In the following example, I used it to remove the reflections in Meagan's glasses. If you've never used it, click on *Help* in the Photoshop or Photoshop Elements menu bar to get information.

POSTERIZATION

Posterizing an image is one way to prepare a photo for stitching that is especially helpful when you make your first Thread Stories quilts. It is a photo-editing technique that reduces the number of colors. This will make it easier to select the colors that you will begin working with.

This process groups together similar colors in patches. For example, the flesh tones in a face are generally the same color. By using the lowest level of posterization, you allow only one or two colors to be seen; another three or four colors are visible as shadows. As the posterization level increases, more color tones are seen, resulting in a smoother gradation. As you get more comfortable with the Thread Stories technique, you can choose to skip the posterization process. The goal is for you to determine the thread colors with your eye as your guide.

Let's start with this photo. If you already have photo-editing software, you can work on a photo of your choice as you follow along.

1. Open a photo that you want to work on in Photoshop Elements. From the menu bar, click *Layer*; then select *New Adjustment Layer* from the drop-down menu and select *Posterize*.

2. In the *New Layer* box, enter the name of the layer. In this example the name is Carmela. Click *OK* to move to the next screen, which shows the posterization levels.

The posterization effect is seen as "clumps" of color in this photograph, which shows posterization level 4.

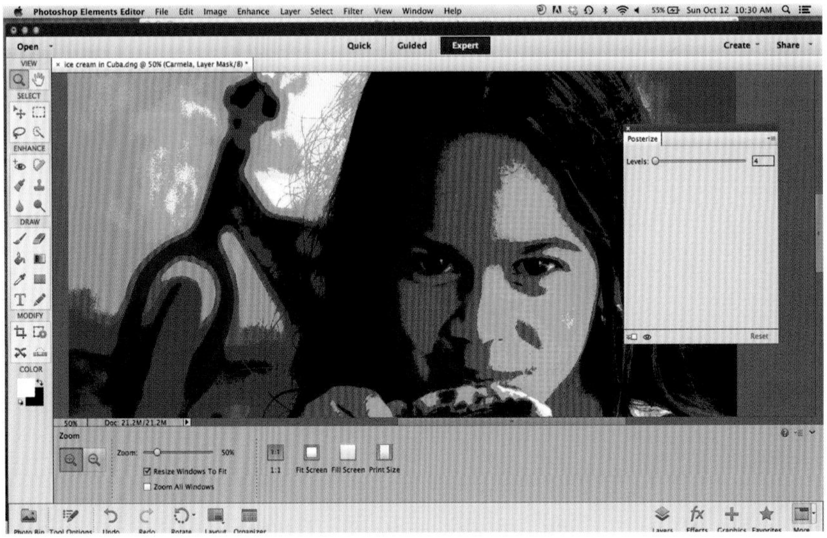

3. As the level of posterization increases, more details become apparent in Carmela's face. At level 8, the shadows and highlights on her face are more pronounced.

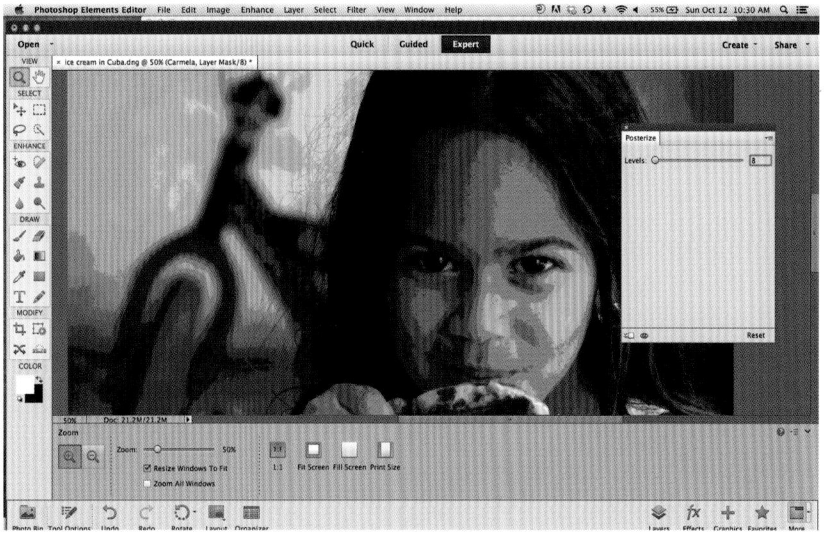

At level 15 there are more colors on her face. The colors are very close to each other. Now you can begin to see how your selection of thread colors can result in a blended finished product.

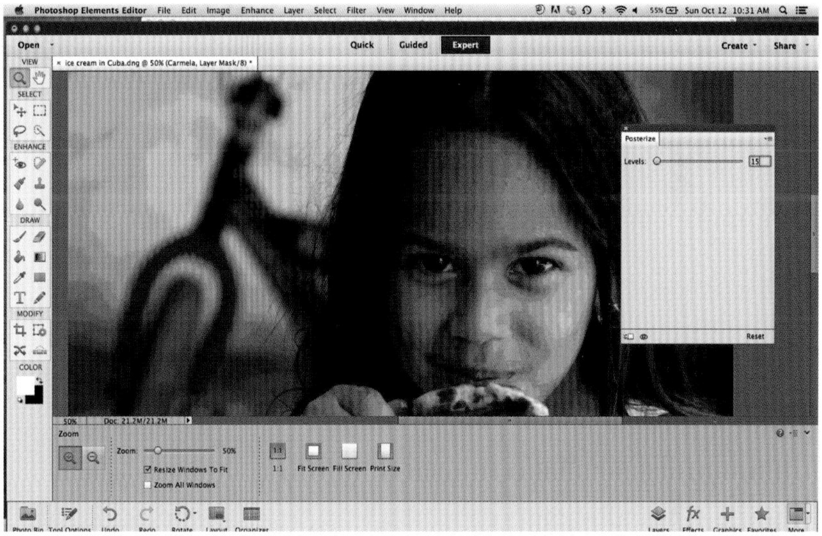

At level 22 the colors blend together very smoothly. This is a good place to stop the posterization process. Once the stitching begins, the goal will be to blend the threads together and remove the lines between specific colors.

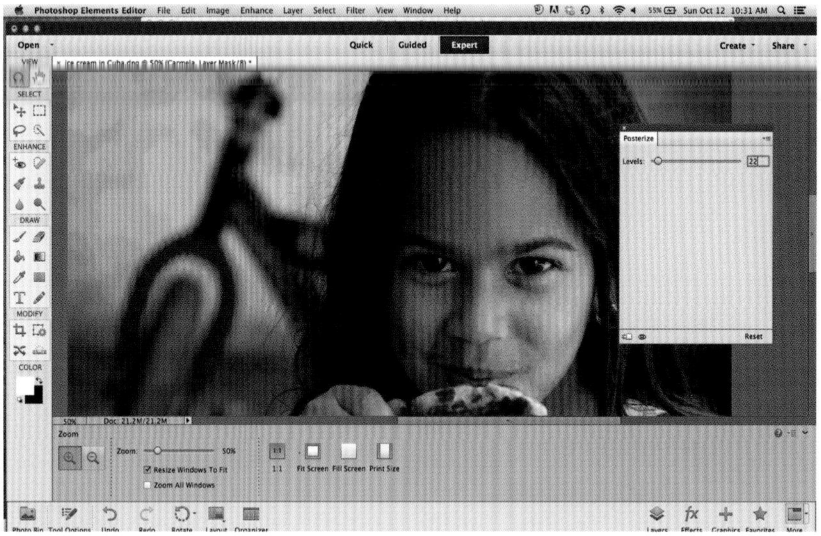

note

The exact level of posterization needed will depend on the photograph. The posterization process is a road map that will allow you to begin to see the colors of thread that need to be selected to achieve blending (see More Posterization Examples, page 29).

4. Save the image with posterization by selecting *File* from the menu bar. Then select *Save*.

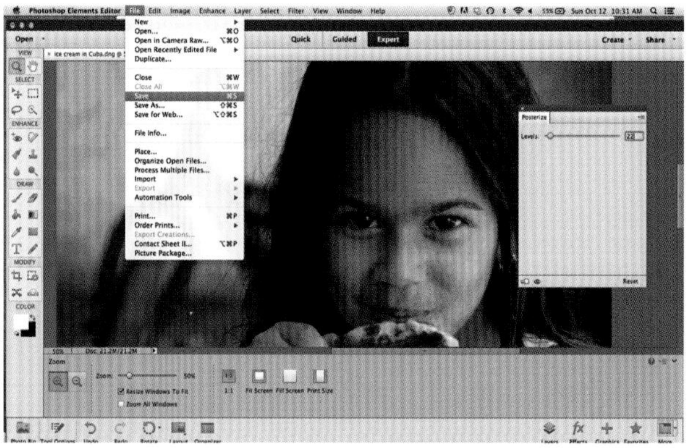

5. After the image has been saved, resize it in a high-resolution format at the size you want your portrait to be. The higher the resolution of the photograph, the more information will be available to you when you start the thread-painting process.

From the menu bar, click on *Image*, select *Resize* from the drop-down menu, and then select *Image Size*.

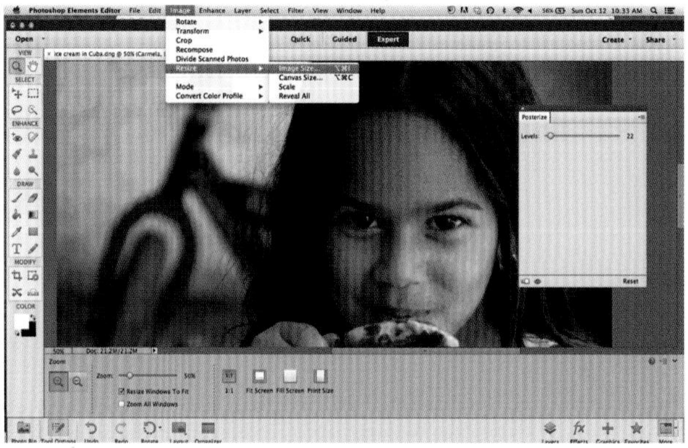

In the *Image Size* screen, make sure the *Scale Styles*, *Constrain Proportions*, and *Resample Image* boxes are checked.

Enter either the *Width* or *Height* that you want (the program will calculate the second dimension to keep the image in proportion).

Enter 300 (pixels per inch) for the resolution.

From the drop-down menu at the bottom of the *Image Size* screen, select *Bicubic Smoother* (best for enlargement).

Click *OK*.

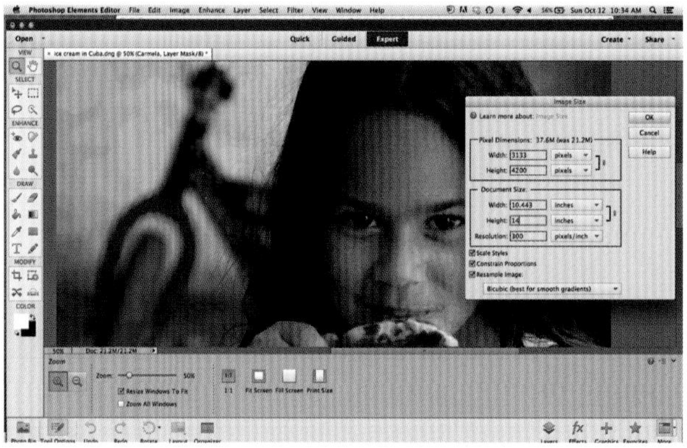

6. The final step is to save the photograph. From the menu bar, click on *File*; then select *Save As* from the drop-down menu. Select *.jpg* from the file options. Another screen will appear that has JPG options. Set the quality to 10 or 12. Click *OK* and you are done.

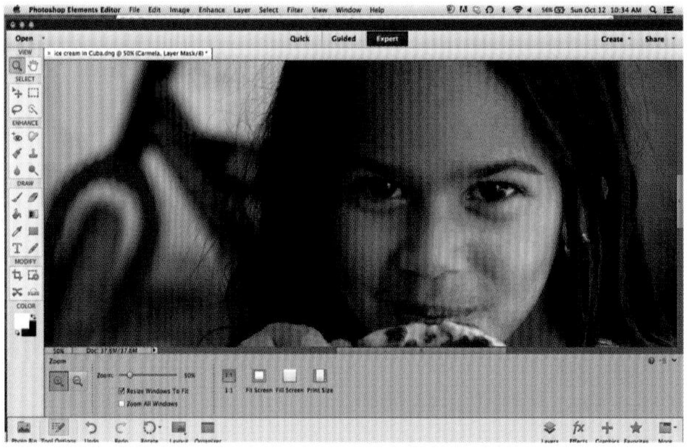

More Posterization Examples

Many factors will affect the level of posterization that works best for you. Even if you adjusted the photograph before you posterized it, you may need to do some final adjustments after posterization to get the photo exactly the way you want it.

The following photographs of Meagan have been posterized. Because of her fair skin, the highlights are extremely light and without texture. As the level of posterization increases, the highlights become more muted, and the final photograph is perfect for stitching.

The exposure of the photograph also affects how much posterization is required to determine the thread colors. The following photograph of Dakota was taken in shadow with the Grand Canyon in the background. He has faded into the background and is not as prominent as desired.

Be careful to make sure your final posterized image is not too dark. Deep tones will lead you to select threads that are too dark for a successful portrait. Adjusting the exposure may result in a more dynamic portrait. After you have successfully adjusted the exposure, clarity, contrast, and saturation, you can select flesh-tone threads with confidence, knowing that your thread-painted subject will be very realistic.

The subject of the photo is too dark and blends into the background.

Better exposure yields a more dynamic photo.

Detail from *Dream Music* (see full quilt, page 102)

Early in my quilting career, I would posterize a photograph and follow the specific colors with my stitching. This resulted in a blocky finished product. This was an acceptable end result for me, because my quilts are typically viewed from across the room and distance softens the lines on the quilt. *Dream Music* was a very out-of-focus photograph taken as this young girl moved while playing her music. Her features are softer than if the photograph had been in full focus.

Detail from *Abuela* (see full quilt, page 101)

Abuela was the third quilt I ever made. Posterization is quite obvious in the subject's cheeks. I posterized the photo at level 9. If I were to posterize it again, I would increase the level to 18, softening the tones of her face.

TIP

You can read about another approach to using the posterization process in Leni Levinson Wiener's book *Pictorial Art Quilt Guidebook: Secrets to Capturing Your Photos in Fabric*. In her book, Leni walks you through the process of using a free photo-editing program called GIMP to create appliqué patterns for portraits.

printing on fabric

After you have selected and edited your photo, you need to print it on paper-backed fabric that is treated to make inkjet ink more permanent. The paper backing stabilizes the fabric so it will easily go through an inkjet printer.

TYPES OF FABRIC

A number of quality brands of paper-backed fabric are readily available in retail stores and online (refer to Resources, page 111, for a list of products and where to buy them). These products are designed to be used with inkjet printers. You cannot use them in any other type of printer.

You'll see that many types of paper-backed fabrics are available. These range from cottons to linens to silks and more. I recommend high-thread-count cotton broadcloth or, if you want more texture in the background, a 5.5-ounce Belgian linen.

EQ Printables and Jacquard Inkjet Fabrics provide paper-backed fabrics in sizes to fit a standard printer, at 8½″ × 11″, and sizes 11″ × 17″ and 13″ × 19″ for wide-format printers. A wide selection of fabrics is available. This product is available in many quilt stores and is also available online.

I use Jacquard Inkjet Fabrics with the FabriSign coating. These fabrics can be printed on using any inkjet printer and will be water resistant but not washable. Jacquard has more than 50 different fabrics to choose from.

If you want to experiment a bit, you can purchase a sample set of fabrics for a nominal fee. This will allow you to see and feel the fabrics and make a decision as to which are best for your project.

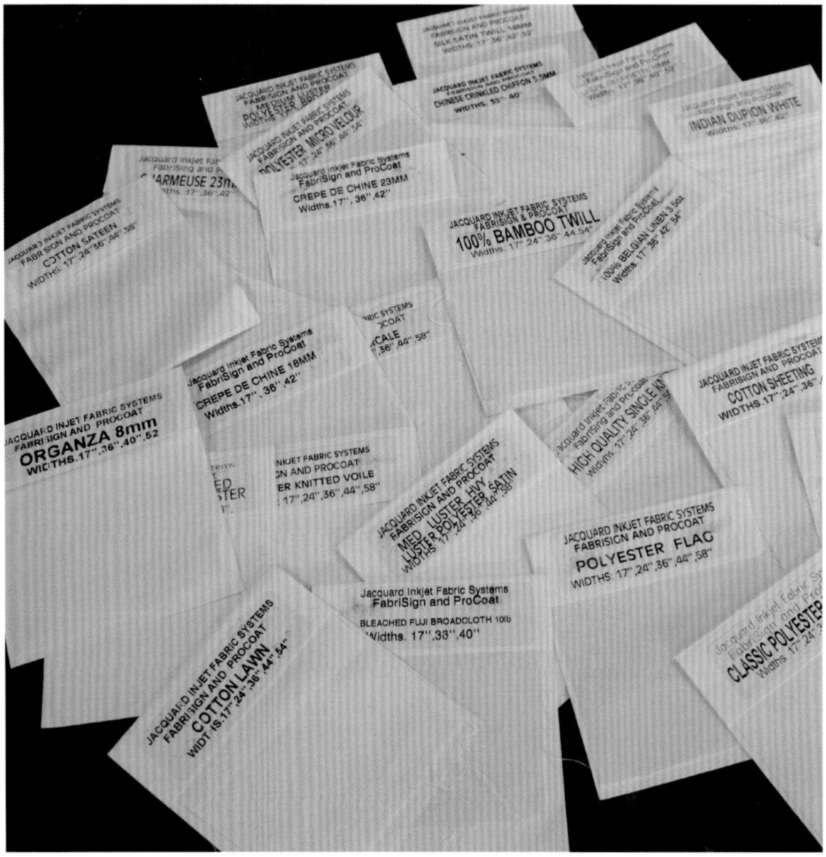

SIZE OF FABRIC

The ready-to-print fabrics come in many forms. Sheets that are 8½″ × 11″ are readily available in quilt and craft stores and online. With this size you can either incorporate your stitched fabric into a larger quilt or print multiple sheets and sew them together for a larger quilt (see Poster Printing, below).

If you have a wider-format printer, you can buy larger sheets or rolls of prepared fabric. Many of my quilts are printed on fabric from a 42″-wide roll of fabric. If I want a larger format, I can turn my image sideways and print an image that is 42″ high by several feet wide.

You can also send your photograph to a company that specializes in printing on fabric (see Resources, page 111).

The paper backing that stabilizes the fabric is easy to remove after the photo has been printed.

Note: Remember to remove the paper backing. It is not a disaster if you forget, but the stitching will be easier if you remove it.

POSTER PRINTING

If you have a large image that you want to print on your home inkjet printer, your inkjet printer may offer poster printing. Look at the available printer options or use the help function. With many printers it's under *Enlarge/Reduce* or *Multi-page*.

This function will break up your image so that it fits on multiple sheets of paper or fabric.

Before printing on your prepared fabric, test the functionality using paper and fast/low-quality black-and-white printing. When you are happy with the results, print your photo on the prepared fabric, making sure that the printer settings are on color and standard quality. Remove the paper backing. Do not sew these sheets of fabric together. Lay them side by side and baste them to the backing cloth. If sewn, a line will appear under the threads that will render the quilt unusable.

getting started

Larry by Jennifer Day, 34″ × 40″, 2013

MAKING A QUILT SANDWICH

Refer to Tools and Supplies (page 9) as needed.

To prepare for stitching, make a quilt sandwich of a photograph printed on fabric, 15-ounce canvas, batting (if you will be hand stitching a binding to the finished quilt), and backing cloth.

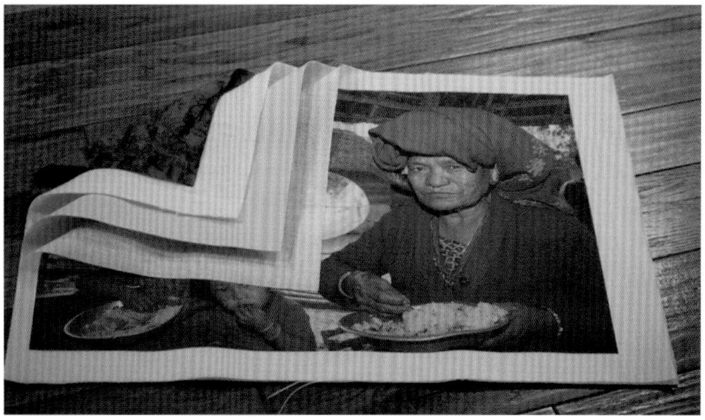

BLENDING IS KEY

The most critical component of this technique is blending: mixing thread colors so there is a gentle and gradual transition from one area of color to another. The key to this process is the smoothing of edges, shapes, and colors to create seamless gradations from one tone to the next so there are no discernible, sharp divisions apparent between colors of thread.

Because you are using thread instead of paint, the process is different than painting. Threads are static, but they can be blended together to create a third color. Layering one on top of another creates texture that will trick the viewer's eye into perceiving a third color (see Blending Skin Tones, page 48).

Realism is an approach to art in which subjects are depicted in as straightforward and realistic a manner as possible. After you have layered and blended the threads, the quilt will have a realistic appearance. Viewers will perceive your art as a painting until they are very close to the quilt. Attention to the blending of threads results in an accurate rendition of the photograph in thread.

Detail from *Larry* (see full quilt, page 34)

An easy way to see how threads blend together is to do some tests on a fabric that closely matches the colors on your printed photo. In this case I have chosen a medium flesh-tone fabric to test threads for a face. The upper left square is stitched with a color similar to the fabric. The upper right is stitched with a slightly lighter tone. Another lighter tone is added to the lower right square, and a final, lightest tone is stitched over all the threads in the lower left quadrant. It is easy to see how this type of blending is done. It is easiest to blend from dark to light. If you try to blend the opposite way, the dark stitching will be readily apparent and not blended.

Often, I will allow the background fabric to show through the threads. You will need to make a decision about the intensity of the stitching on each of your quilts. Interestingly, when you are stitching over an area that has a gradation of color in the photograph, the thread will begin to visually change color and take on the hue of the cloth color beneath the threads. The absorption of the color of the photograph in the threads will allow you to stitch less intensely.

These are the four threads used on this practice piece.

This nose was created using the same threads as in the practice square of fabric. The darkest thread is at the tip of the nose, with the lighter threads radiating out from there. The nostril and curvature of the nose are in a darker thread.

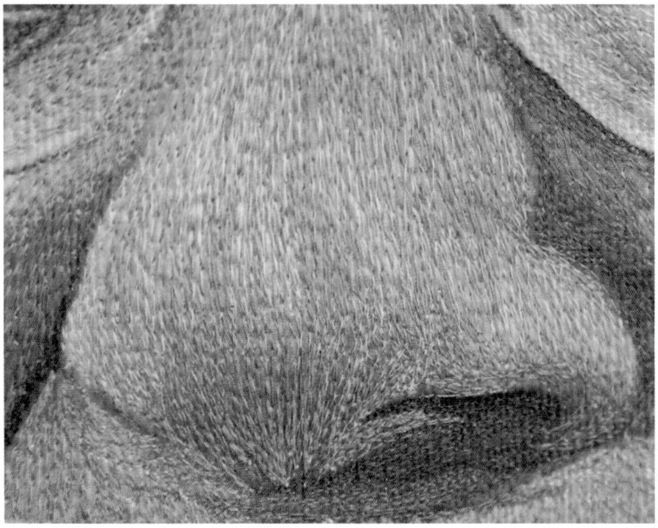

Detail from *Judy* (see full quilt, page 110)

In *When I Was Young*, the same thread tones are used along with a bit of purple added in the crease of the elbow. I stitched the darkest flesh tone first, then the purple. The lighter skin tones were then applied over the first two colors, creating this blended look.

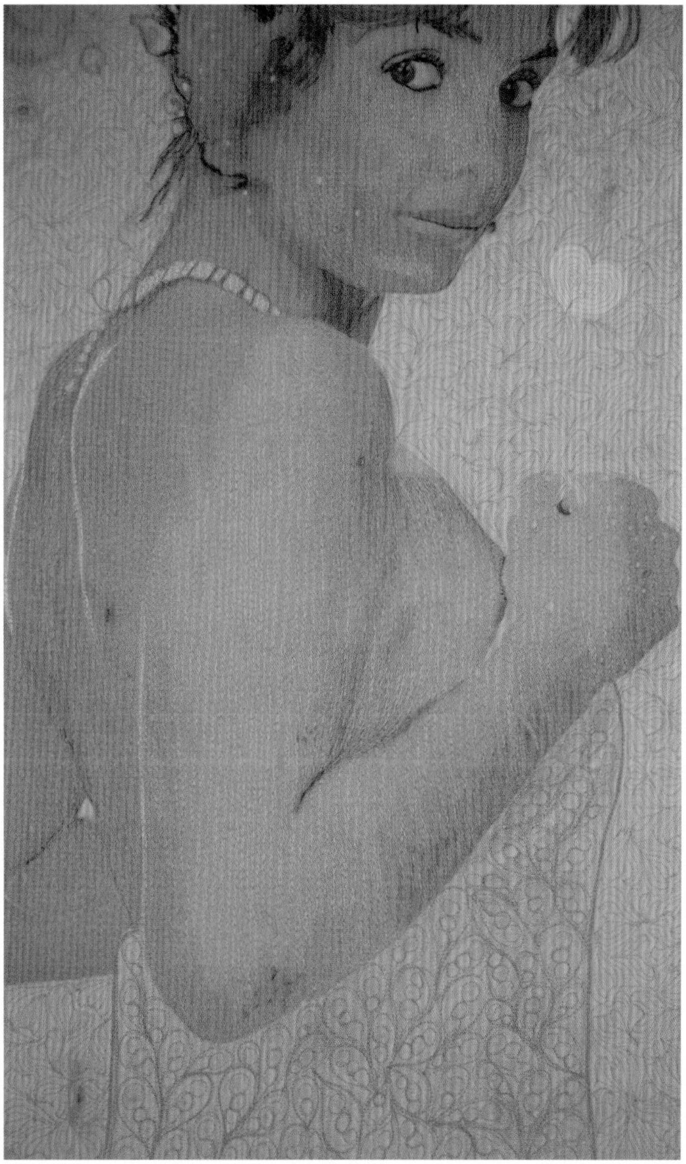

Notice the purple tinge in the crease of the elbow.

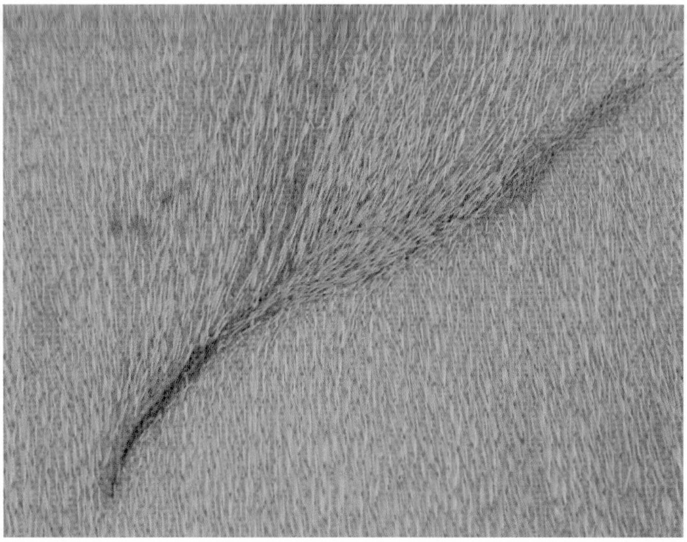

Details from *When I Was Young* (see full quilt, page 104)

STITCHING DIRECTION

I try to stitch the majority of my artworks in a vertical pattern. If there is a curve to the face or anatomy, I will stitch following the curve of the body. This is evident in the tip of the nose and the nostril of the boy (right), as well as the crease of the arm (see detail of elbow from *When I Was Young*, page 37). Following the curve of a cheekbone gives grace and realism to the image.

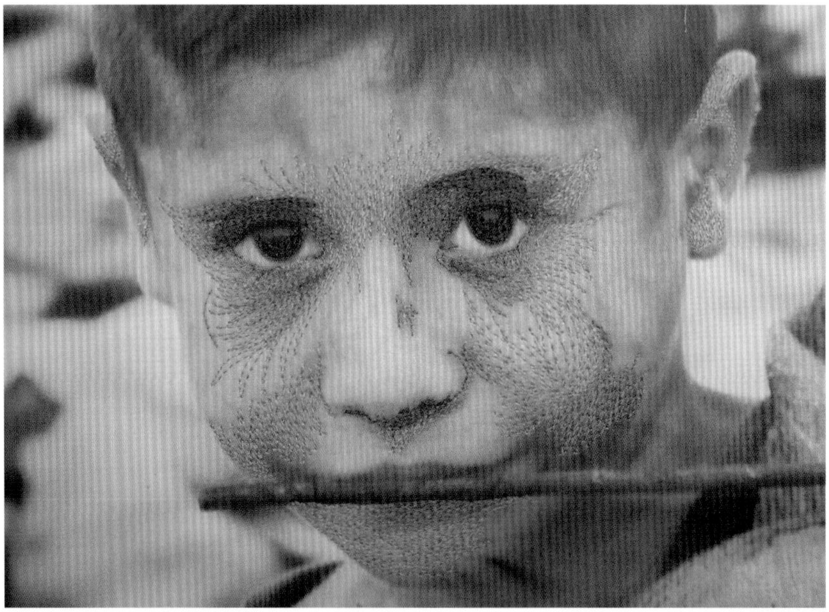

The stitching follows the curve of the cheek.

One of the most fun things to do in thread painting is creating hair. Hair moves in crazy patterns, and it is important to follow the wisps and curves to create a lifelike portrait. *Wisdom* was my fourth quilt. Donald was 84 years old when I took the photograph. By the time I finished stitching his hair and beard, I was ready to take him to the barbershop!

Detail from *Wisdom* (see full quilt, page 59)

Early in my career I made a quilt of my son, using the zigzag stitch on my sewing machine. This is an interesting approach to thread painting. The end product is not as realistic as a quilt using straight stitches, but there may be a time when you require more texture in your finished piece and want to use the zigzag technique.

I Didn't Do It...! by Jennifer Day, 24″ × 26″, 2010

It is important to realize that, to the observer's eye, the color of the thread can change depending on the color below the thread. In this quilt, *Cuban Ballerina*, I used a green thread. You can see its true color below the step on the left. The thread mimics the intensity of the green color printed on the fabric beneath it. The green behind the stair rail is more muted and the color in other areas appears three shades lighter. Applying the thread lightly allows the photograph's color beneath it to impact the hue that is perceived by the viewer. This allows you to make short work of color application. I finished all of the green thread application in this 14″ × 16″ area of the quilt in under an hour, with 64 thread snips as I moved the needle to different locations to apply the thread.

Detail from *Cuban Ballerina* (see full quilt, page 109)

There is only one green thread and one gold thread used in this detail. The underlying color is clearly mimicked by the gold thread, causing the viewer's eye to see several different colors in this small area. Keeping the threads less densely stitched creates success with this technique.

the eyes have it

Los Mambesis by Jennifer Day, 38″ × 32″, 2012

There is an old English proverb, "The eyes are the window to the soul." This saying stems from a passage in the Bible, Matthew 6:22–23. A form of this quote has been traced back to Cicero, who lived from the year 106 B.C. until 43 B.C. Many different poets have used this proverb, including William Shakespeare.

Pay a great deal of attention to the eyes when you are photographing your subjects because they have a significant effect on the overall portrait.

The eyes are the main focus in portraits because they tell us so much about the subject. The emotions of anger, disappointment, curiosity, fear, hope, happiness, love, lust, sadness, or surprise are all in the eyes.

Las Mambesis (page 40) is based on a photograph I took of an old man on the plaza in Havana, Cuba. "Las Mambesis" refers to the guerilla Cuban independence soldiers who fought against Spain in the Ten Years' War (1868–1878). This man would have been in his 30s in 1959 when the United States broke off relations with Cuba—maybe his hat is a comment on international relations. He is now a musician playing his instrument in the plaza, free for all to hear. Although there is only a faint smile on his lips, there is a wonderful light in his eyes.

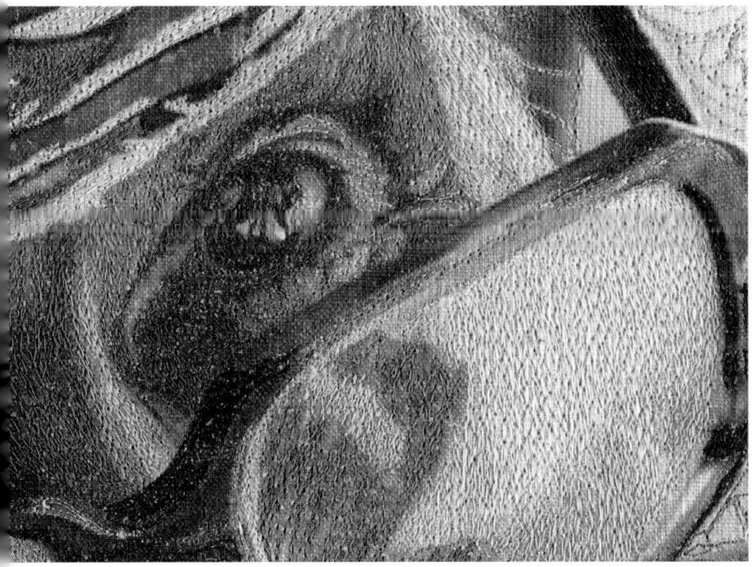

Detail from *Las Mambesis* (see full quilt, page 40)

The very first thing you should stitch on a portrait quilt is the eye. If you make a mistake capturing the soul of the individual, you must start over. Better to know sooner rather than later!

THE IRISES

The iris is the portion of the eye that has color. There are many ways to approach depicting the iris of the eye. The key is to find the colors that will draw the viewer in. The iris of an eye is very complex—it contains many speckles or blotches of color. Often two or three colors of thread are needed to complete the coloration of the iris. Think about incorporating embroidery thread to provide a sheen, much like the gloss that a real eye has due to the moisture in it.

Detail from *Cuban Guitar* (see full quilt, page 102)

The pattern of threads in the eye can be circular or radiating. Both applications are beautiful. The choice is yours.

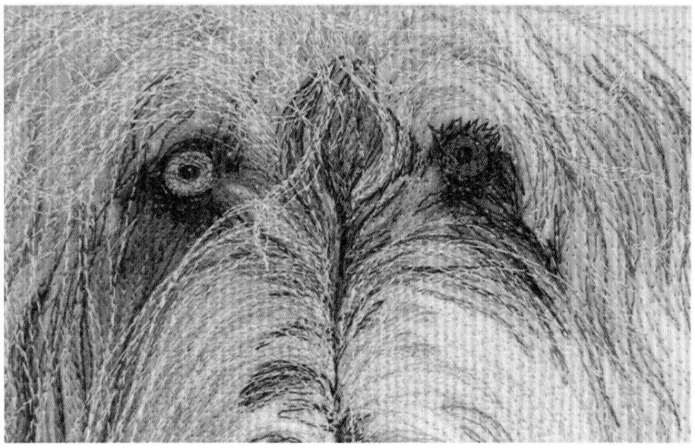

Detail from *B Bear* by Mary Zahner (see full quilt, page 95)

Eyes created with a circular motion

THE WHITES

In a portrait, I prefer to leave the whites of the eyes, and many times the pupils, without thread. Leaving these areas untouched will give a luminescence to the individual's eyes. Another reason for leaving the whites alone is that the whites are rarely white. They have almost as many hues as the iris. Older people may have a bit of pink and even gray around the iris.

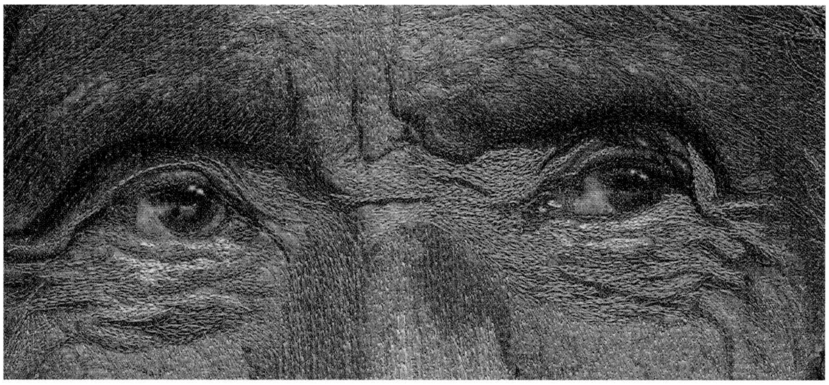

Detail from *Grace* (see full quilt, page 65)

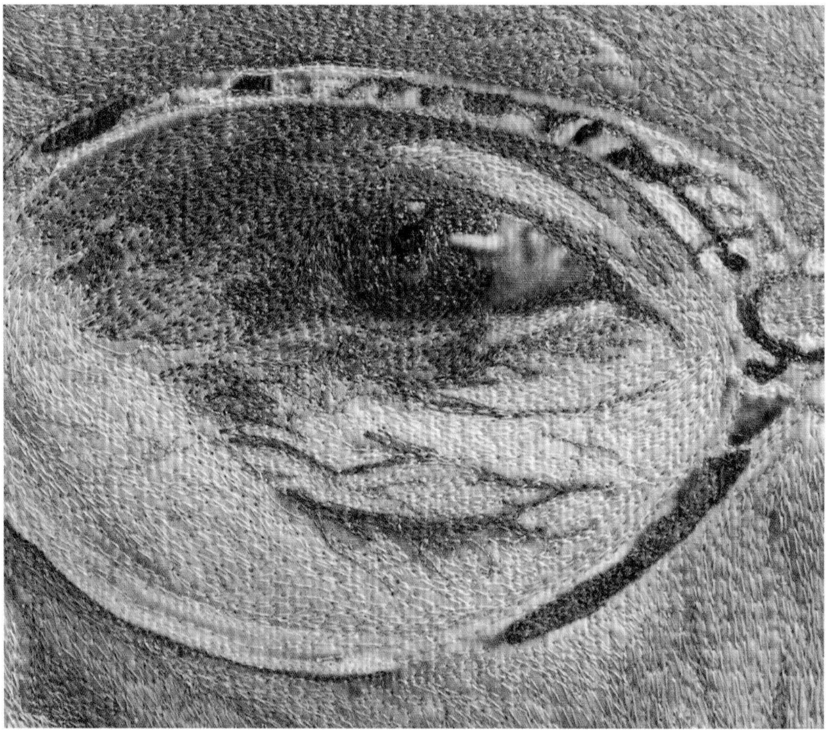

Detail from *Judy* (see full quilt, page 110)

Young adults and children will have the whitest eyes, and this lends an air of innocence to their portraits. Again, the eyes tell the story.

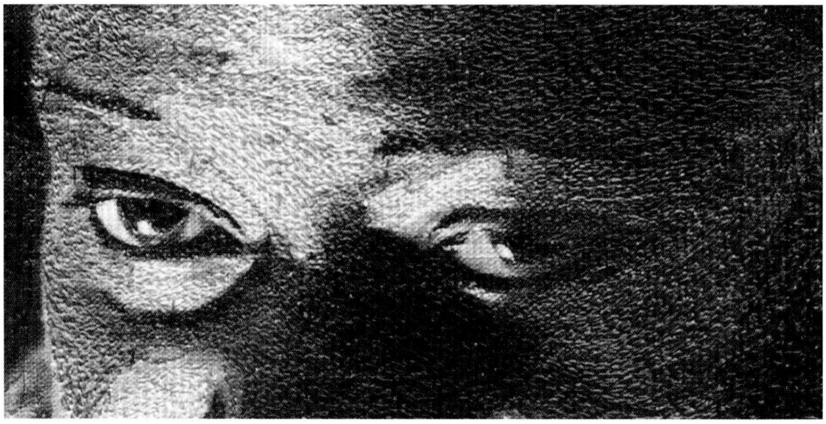

Detail from *Let There Be Light* (see full quilt, page 5)

The following quilts are of the same child. One has the whites filled in with thread, while the other does not. Seeing the original photograph next to the quilt that is 100 percent covered in thread shows a startling contrast in artistic approach.

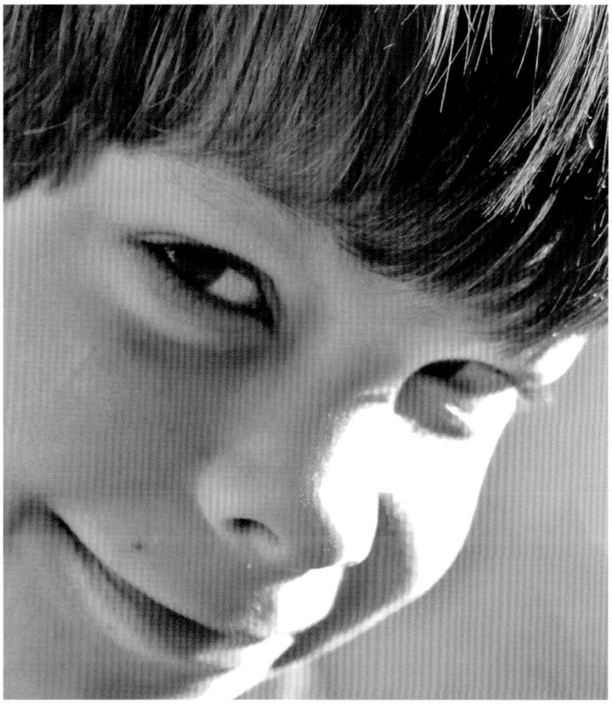

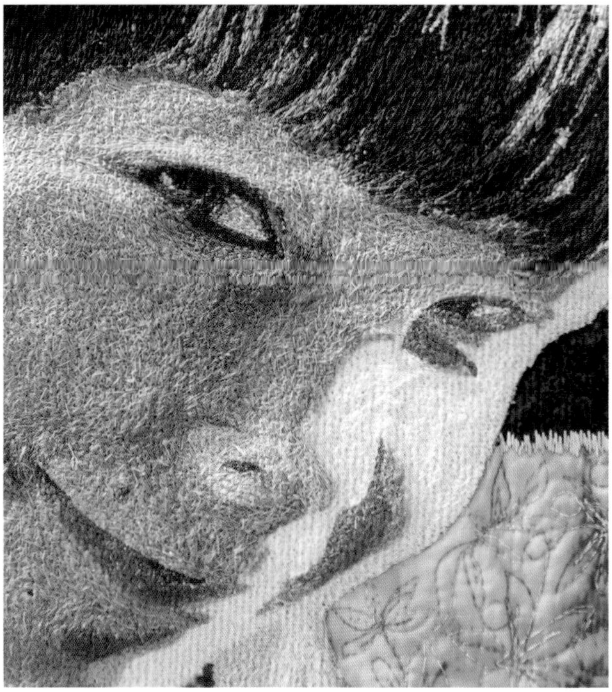

Detail from *I Didn't Do It...!* (see full quilt, page 39)

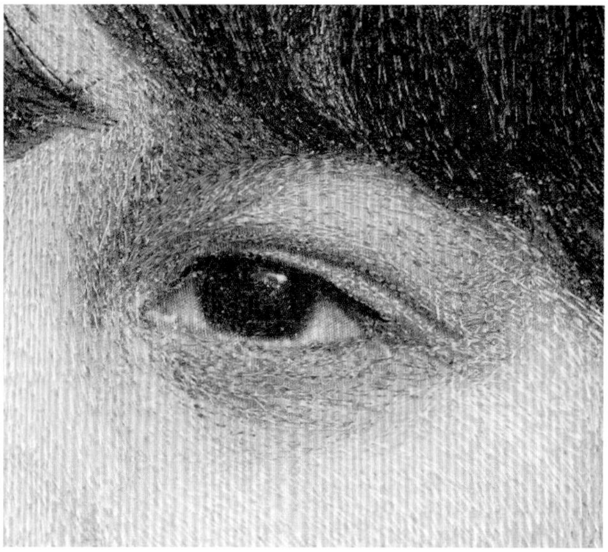

Detail from *Carson and the Barn Cat* (see full quilt, page 109)

The eye of the old man in the detail below also has thread in the whites and is not as realistic as it would have been without this treatment. There may be times when you don't stitch the white or the iris because you don't want to draw attention to the area or you want the printed fabric to show through.

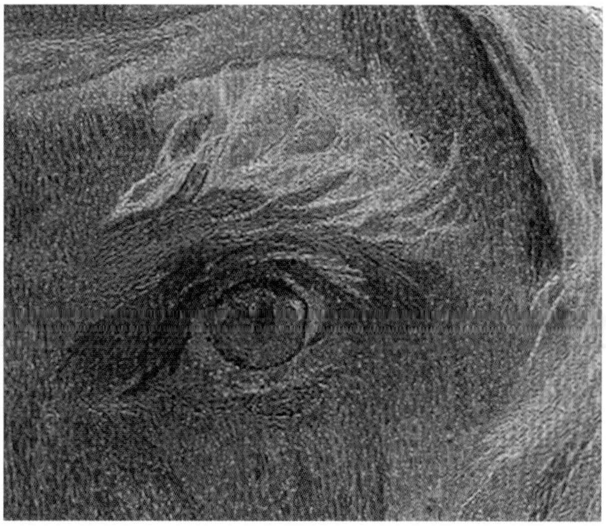

Detail from *Wisdom* (see full quilt, page 59)

Totally covering the individual's eye and face with stitching creates more of a posterized art image versus a finished product that is very realistic. There is room in the art world for both concepts. This, again, is within your realm of choice.

BEGIN STITCHING THE EYES

Note: As an experienced thread artist, I did do some stitching on the hair with the dark thread. As a beginner, you should always start with the eyes.

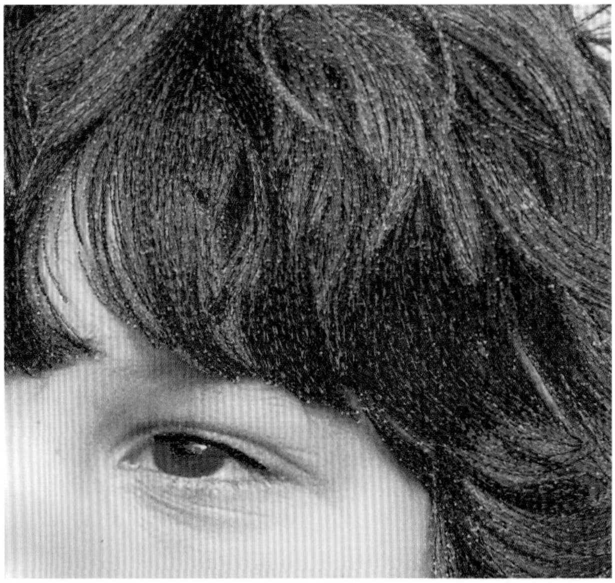

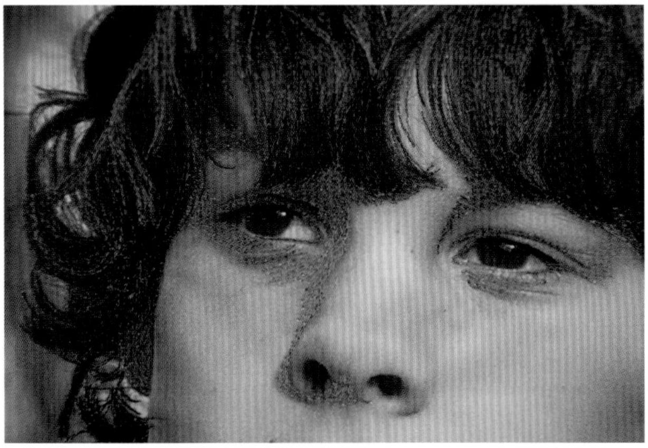

1. To begin the stitching process with the eye, a bit of outlining is the first move. Always thread paint the tones from darkest to lightest. For this child's eye, the very dark line at the eyelash and the pupil is the place to start stitching.

2. Finish outlining the eye with thread; then add the medium brown tone that is a shadow reflective of the hair tones above the eyes.

3. Next, stitch the darker skin color around and under the eye and along the nose, creating shadows. Blending this third tone over the eyelid and below the eye puts the finishing touch on the eye. The subject has life and the stitching is successful. Now you can begin to work on the rest of the face, adding texture and shadows where needed.

TIP

In this example, I stitched only the pupil and not the iris. I liked the glint in the boy's eye and thought it would look best unstitched. This is something you learn by trial and error.

Highlights

I always leave the glint of highlight (a white spot in the eye that is a reflection of light) in the eye unstitched. In the dog's eye, the highlights are very soft. They almost match the luminescence in the white of the eye. Filling the highlight with a white thread will confuse the viewer.

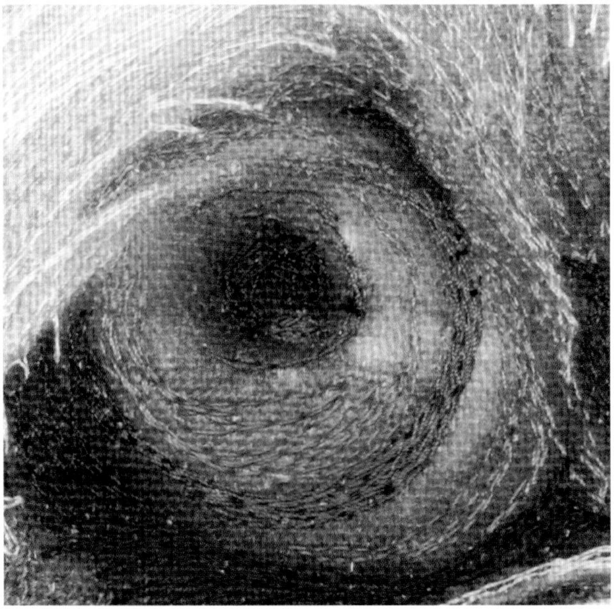

Detail from student work of *B Bear* (see full quilt, page 95)

The elderly woman in the quilt detail at right has a highlight that is more typical of most photographs. This is a clear bright light in the eye that needs to be left alone. This light gives the eye a shimmer that creates a spark of interest that is critical to the success of the portrait. It is also interesting to note that the old woman has cataracts. The thin line of gray blue thread around her brown iris tells another tale.

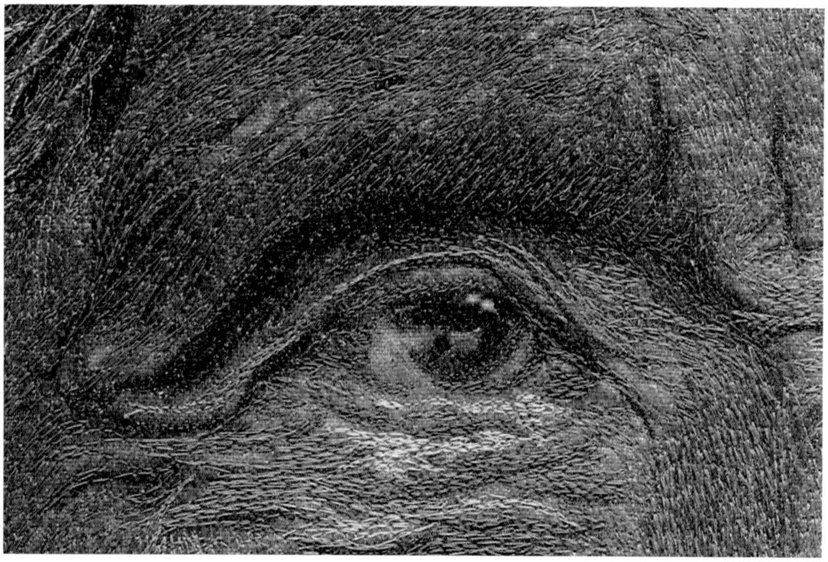

Detail from *Grace* (see full quilt, page 65)

As you work the area around the eye, you'll be making decisions about areas that can be left unstitched. The white of the old man's eye (right) is unstitched, as is a small crease both above and below his eye. The area below the shadow under his eye and the area between the eye and nose are very lightly stitched. The original fabric is visible in these areas.

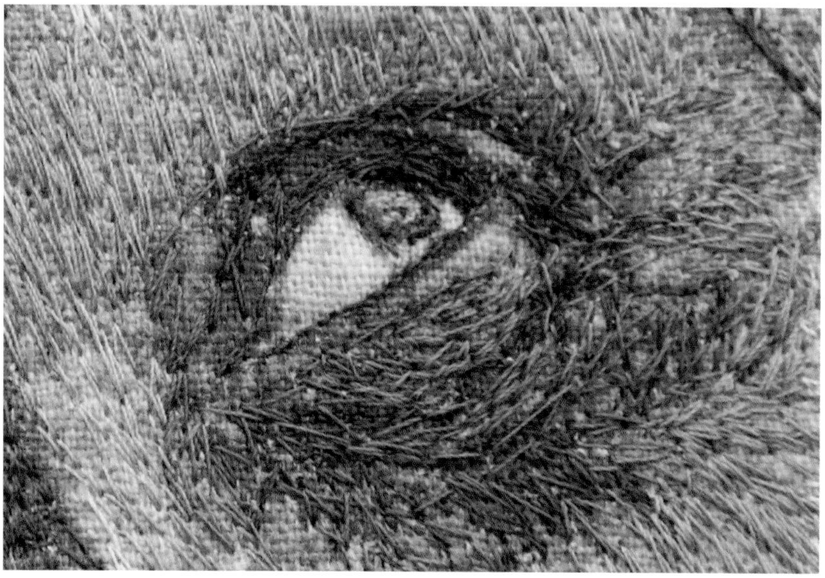

Detail from *Cuban Guitar* (see full quilt, page 102)

It's always up to you to decide what parts of the eye to stitch. I chose not to stitch the cat's eye in the quilt detail depicted at right because there are so many colors in the iris. If I had added thread in this area, the image would appear muddled and lose its clarity. I also left the tiny reflective lights along the black surrounding the eye. These could easily have been lost in stitching, but it is more interesting to see the light in these areas.

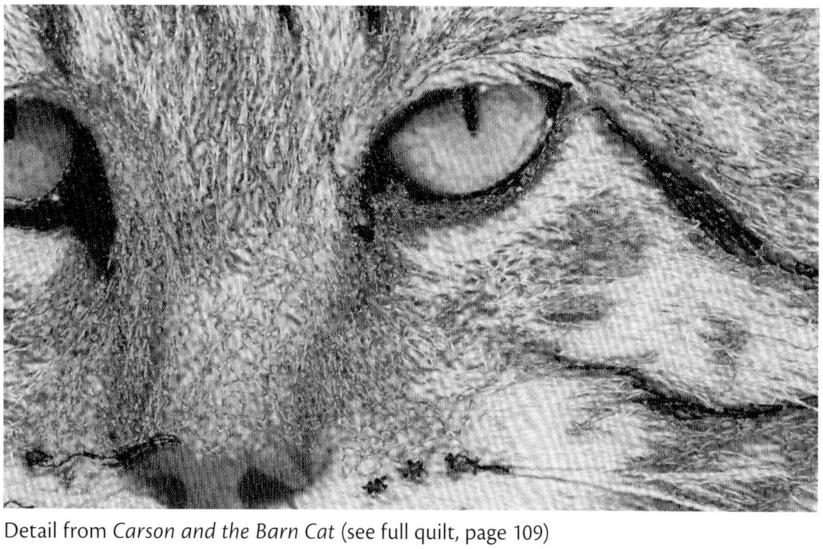

Detail from *Carson and the Barn Cat* (see full quilt, page 109)

Eyelashes

Eyelashes are a major design element to address in a portrait. I did not add lashes to any of the eyes on the quilts in the previous examples, with the exception of the young woman in *Let There Be Light*. Even her lashes were restricted to one or two at the most.

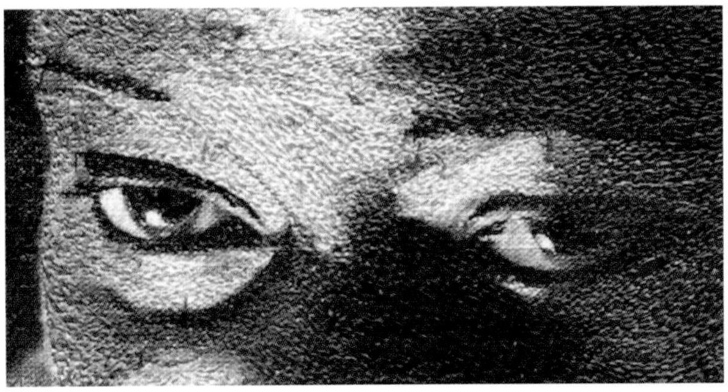

Detail from *Let There Be Light* (see full quilt, page 5)

Eyelashes are most critical in young children, girls in particular. I prefer to stitch the eyelashes in one line of stitching. This adds an almost ethereal appearance to the child. This calls for a lot of starts and stops and thread cutting, but it is worth it in the end.

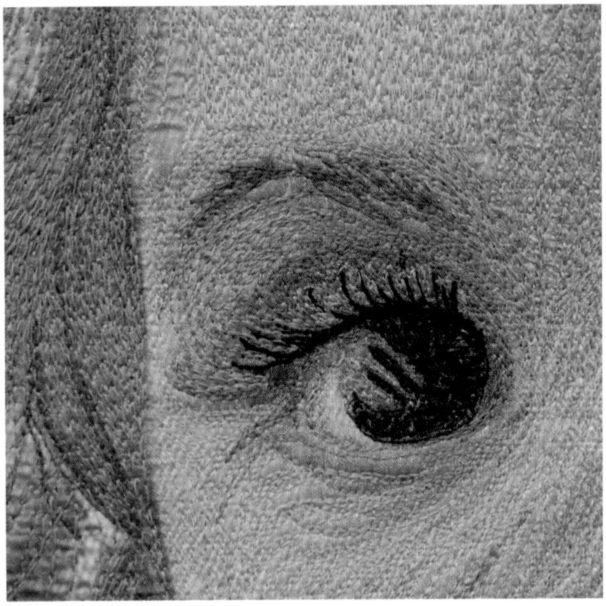

Detail from *Mmm...Good* (see full quilt, page 107)

Since you cannot see Alex's eyes in the quilt below, the lashes become a large part of the story. Her downcast expression is important to the tale being told, as her attention is on the column of threads that are stacked on top of a stash of fabric at her feet. I started the line of stitching at her lid and placed one line of thread over her lashes and then cut the thread. Each lash is an individual row of stitching. As I added the threads of her skin, I stitched over some of the tips of the lashes, giving them a wispier effect.

Beginnings by Jennifer Day, 38″ × 36″, 2014

blending skin tones

In this chapter, we'll explore blending skin tones to bring your thread portrait to life.

AUDITIONING THREADS

Auditioning threads is the first step in this creative art quilt process. This process involves carefully examining your threads and selecting those that most closely match the skin tones in your photograph. Place each thread you are considering over the area that you want to match. It is better to choose a color slightly lighter than the color in the photograph because the stitches intensify in color as they are laid down on the fabric. Selecting a lighter hue will ultimately result in an almost perfect match. *Take your time with this process.*

The Mara thread line by Gütermann contains 692 colors. The minute gradation of thread colors is critical to the success of creating a realistic piece of art based on a photograph. The Jennifer Day Thread Stories line of threads offers 144 threads specifically chosen from the Gütermann Mara line for thread-painted portraiture. My Thread Stories set of threads specifically addresses skin and hair color and will work on 90 percent of projects undertaken, but you may need to purchase additional threads to put the finishing touches on your artwork. If the only colors that you have to choose from come from your local quilt store, you will need to collect thread from several different vendors to get the colors you need for your art.

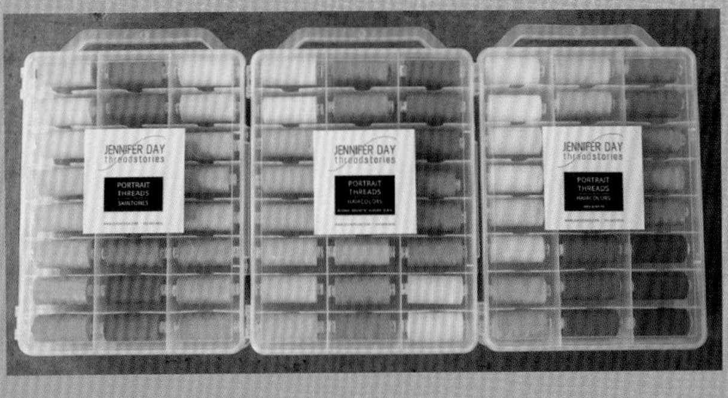

Alex, the little two-year old girl in *Beginnings* (page 47), has skin that is the texture of a newborn.

Through the process of elimination, I chose the six threads in the photo below to start with as I began creating Alex. Adding the rose of her cheeks and lips to the mix in the beginning is important. It is easy to see the three threads on the right blending over the rose tone used as the blush of her cheeks on the left.

With practice you'll train your eye to see subtle color differences and be more able to find threads that mimic the colors in your photographs. We'll walk through layering threads to create a finished portrait so you can see how I do it.

Note: The quilt Beginnings *has not incorporated the posterization process to the photograph. (For more information, see Posterization, page 25.)*

STARTING THE BLENDING PROCESS

Capturing the clear tones of Alex's baby skin in thread is very difficult. In fact, baby skin is the most difficult type of skin to render in thread. But I'm starting the explanation of the treatment of skin with her because it is very easy to see the basic blending steps.

I recommend that you start making thread portraits using photos of older men and women. It takes time to learn the intricacies of thread painting, and with faces of the elderly you can make mistakes and still have a natural-looking result.

Okay, deep breath. Here you go.

1. After you have selected the threads to use in the portrait, sit back and stare at the face. You want to concentrate on seeing the skin's subtle color differences. We'll begin the sewing process by adding the rose tone to the girl's cheek and lips. I almost always work from the darkest thread to the lightest. By starting with the rose tone, you can layer and blend the subsequent threads that will give a glow to her skin. I have purposely left space between the threads so that her cheeks have a suggestion of blush versus a totally red cheek.

2. This next step is scary—adding the next-darkest color. It seems as though the girl's skin will be too dark and orange, but trust me. There are more colors to be added, so it is best to take a deep breath and begin sewing. I do not cover the rose tone on the child's cheek entirely with the second color of thread. I want just a bit of the rose glow peaking through, so I leave space between the threads.

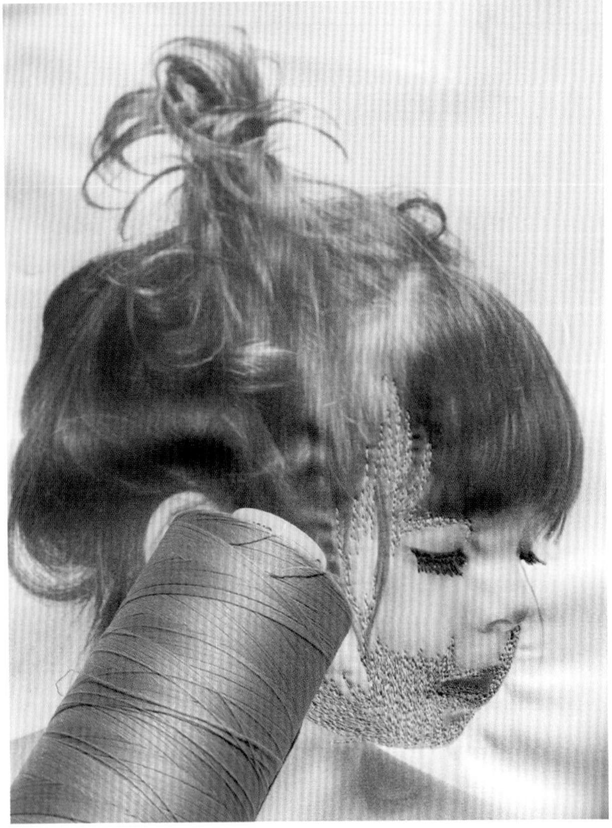

note

It is important to have a photograph of the subject nearby; an unposterized version is best. This allows you to see any areas that have been "lost" in the thread-painting process. By looking at the photograph, you can see how to rescue your work and capture the image perfectly in thread.

Although her nose has a dark color on it, I have not added the thread to the tip of the nose yet. I will do this with the next layer of color so I can make sure the tip of the nose is in the right spot. If I had added it at this stage, I might lose the location of the tip.

3. Next we will stitch a lighter thread tone onto Alex's face. I have chosen a color that is lighter than the fabric for this step. Because thread is three dimensional, it captures light and shadow. These shadows will make the thread look darker. Choosing a lighter thread than the color of the photograph is better at this point in the process.

4. The last color to be added for now is just a bit darker than the previous thread. This is the true moment of blending, as this color is blended over all the other threads. Because it is just a shade darker than the lightest tone, it will blend quite easily. Now the face is coming to life. The shadows created by the other colors are muted as the threads are melded together.

The colors that will be used in the girl's hair will change the perception of her skin tone—the dark brown and the gold highlights will blend with the face threads and bring her countenance to life. Only then will you be able to see how best to proceed with the final facial blending. (We'll cover hair in Hair, page 59.)

Remember, you can create a color by layering threads and tricking the eye into seeing the desired tones, much as you do when using paint.

5. Now that the face and hair are filled in, you can see where you need to begin to make final adjustments. In the next photograph, you can see that I added the shadow under the girl's nose and below her chin. I also added more of the light thread in her cheek. Tendrils of loose hair have been sewn along her neck, giving her a young and carefree look.

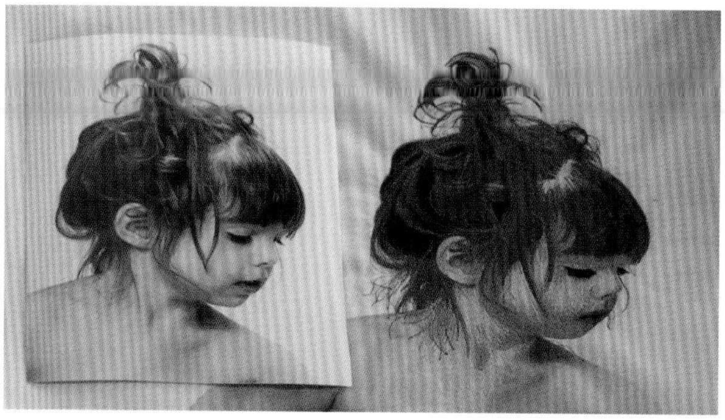

note

It is important to note at this point that no one will see the original photograph unless you are showing it along with the quilt. It is up to you to make the decision as to how far you will go to create an absolutely realistic image. This is where I drive myself crazy spending a few more hours trying to get to that goal line of realism.

TIP

One key to this technique is that if you have thread in an area that is not visually correct, you can add threads over the top of the troubling color and erase the problem. I never use a ripper; I just add more thread!

ELISHA (DIVERSE SKIN TONES)

I broke my own rule about stitching the eyes first on this quilt because this quilt is a teaching tool and I was confident that I could capture Elisha's eyes, as they are small and they don't have much shading around them.

Elisha is from the Dominican Republic. She is hanging her clothes on a line to dry in front of her home, an old abandoned chocolate factory, where the water she uses to clean her clothes comes from a pump in the center of the factory. She is a single mother with three young children and works at a local resort, where she gets paid $15 a day. I was immediately drawn to her because of the fabulous curlers in her hair. My son Carson and I spent quite a bit of time talking to her about her life on the island—I spoke a little bit of Spanish and she spoke a bit of English. She had migrated from Haiti after her then husband had burned their house down to exorcise the demons living there. Another story!

To begin the portrait, I chose to accent Elisha's cheeks, as I did with young Alex (page 49), with a bit of rose tone. This creates a blush and gives depth to her skin. I also chose to add this color to her nostrils to create the shadow along her nose.

note

Let me introduce my catch phrase "sketchy-scratchy." This phrase refers to lightly scribbling an area with thread so that when another layer is applied, you can see bits and pieces of the first layer of thread under the second layer.

The next step is to add some of the flesh tone to Elisha's forehead. This is a slightly darker color than the final color of her skin, which will come with the next color of thread. I purposely stitched a light pattern with this thread. I want a little bit of this color to peak through the next layer, but it should not overpower the next color.

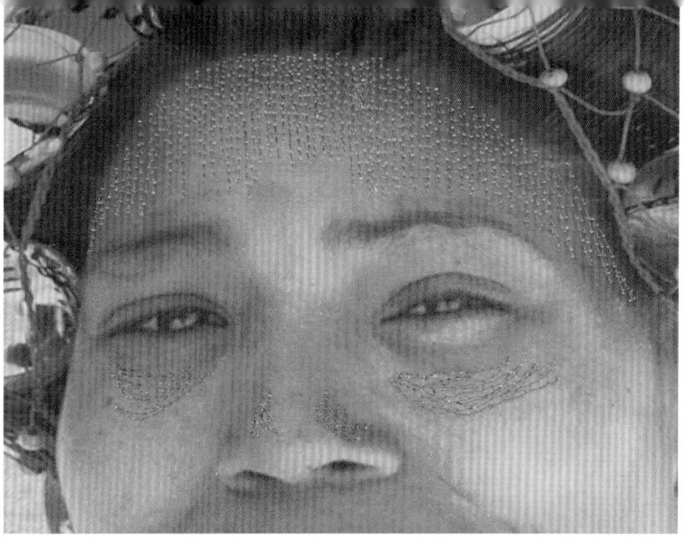

I then place a second color over the top of the first thread on the forehead. I am using the "sketchy-scratchy" technique along the hairline as well as the right side of her forehead so that when the threads of her hair and the shadow of the side of her face are added, they can be blended in with the face threads. Because the photograph has not been posterized (see Posterization, page 25), I have to determine where to start and stop the application of each color. The key is to train your eye to determine the gradations of color. Each time you make a new quilt you will gain more confidence in your abilities and the process of thread selection will go faster.

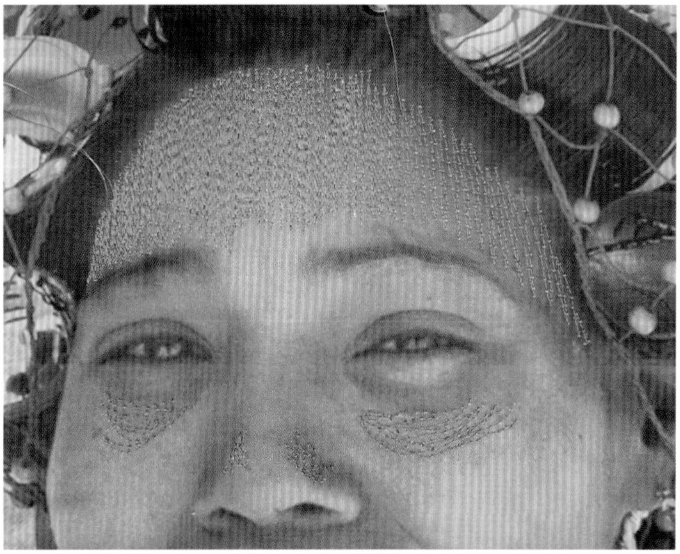

The application of the dark thread around Elisha's eyes and on her irises is straight-forward. I lightly stitched her eyebrows so that when I go back in between the eyebrow hairs with flesh-tone thread, blending will occur.

Now I will add some textural definition to her face. The grooves along the side of her mouth should be stitched before the application of the threads on her cheeks, to avoid losing the location where the darker stitching needs to be placed. The addition of sketchy-scratchy shadowing under the eye and below the eyebrow will define these areas for the next phase.

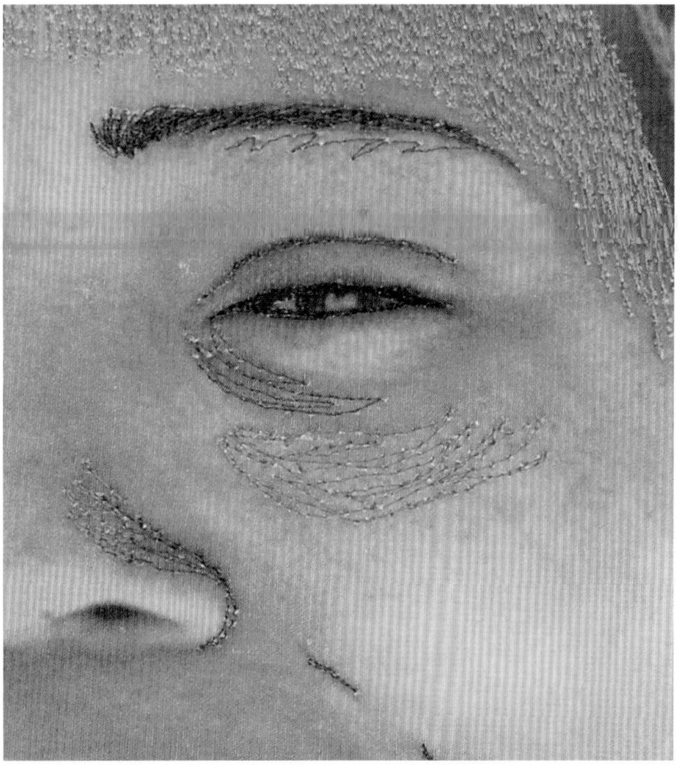

I added more shadows on Elisha's eyelids and below her eyes as well as around her eyebrows. Below her nose there is space left between the threads so that the next layer will blend easily.

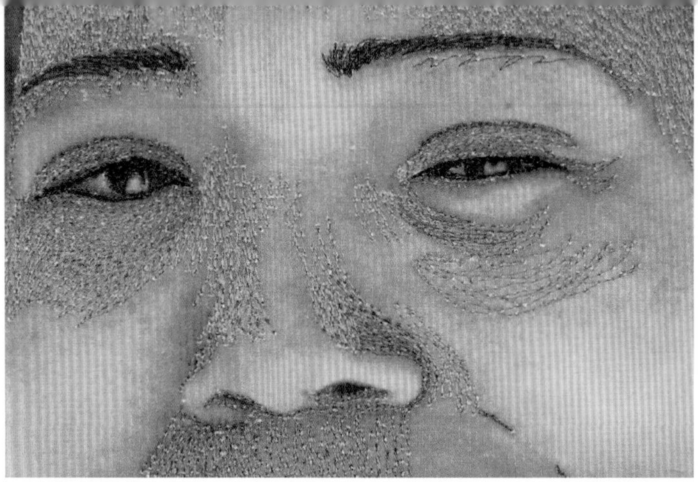

Many times the skin has tones in it that are counterintuitive. There is a purple haze to the bridge of Elisha's nose. This is created by the reflection of light on her face. I want to capture this haze with purple fiber. Again, I audition the thread by laying a strand across her nose over the top of the area that I want to concentrate on. I use a very light application of the purple fiber as a base for the next layer of thread.

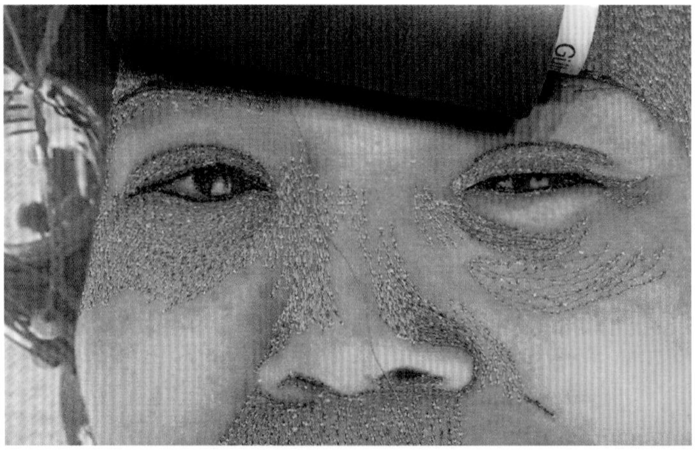

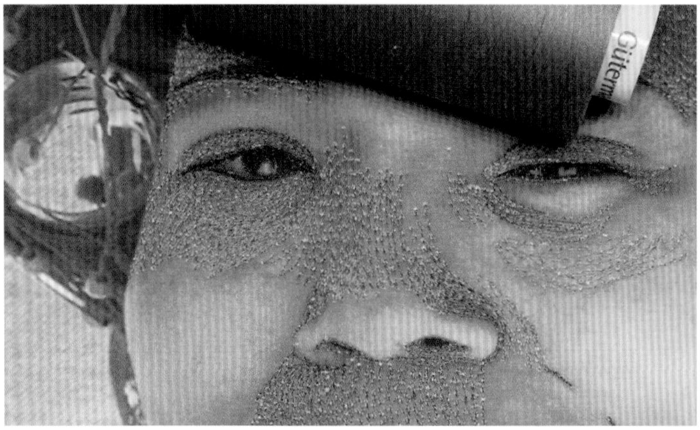

After the next thread is stitched over the purple shadow, you can see where the blush on her cheek will go as well as the shadow under her eye. A lighter color of thread will be applied next to the tip of her nose, cheeks, and eyelid, indicating the high points of her face that reflect light.

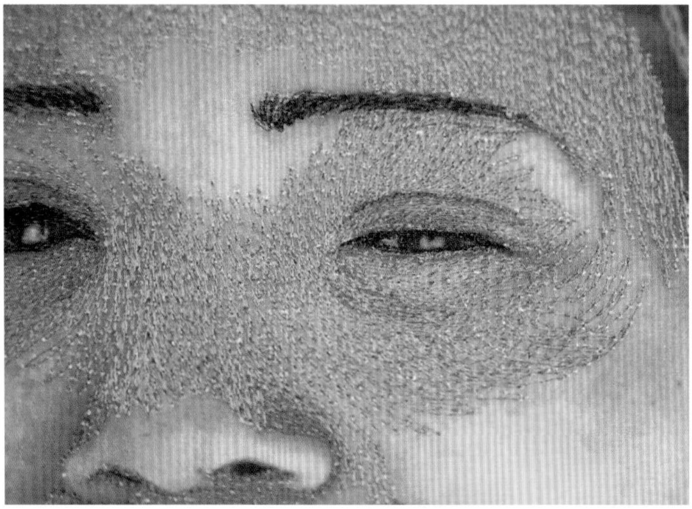

JUDY (ELDERLY SKIN)

I met Judy one day in the checkout line at a grocery store. She is the epitome of a woman balancing her life. Is she working because she enjoys people or because the state of her finances does not meet her needs? I was immediately drawn to the stories that her countenance tells. Her wrinkles are many, but they are also graceful and exhibit her personality. When she smiles, her face lights up with laugh lines.

Creating a portrait quilt of an individual with wrinkles is an amazing journey. A person with age has skin colors ranging from soft cream to brown, as well as from red to purple and even spots of white. As you start and stop stitching in order to move from a wrinkle to an age spot, you may find yourself empathizing with the person you are depicting. One day all of us will have as many spots and creases in our skin. Your art is almost a mirror into the future.

I always create my portraits with all the highlights and blemishes that can be seen in the original photograph. That is why my art is realistic. If an individual wishes to commission my work and wants less character in his or her face, I will decline the assignment. I want to portray people as they really are. Darn, I had better pass on a self-portrait!

Photo for *Judy* (see full quilt, page 110)

Texture

Wrinkles on a face are textural. Each curve, dip, ridge, groove, and furrow is a narrative of a person's life. Wrinkles are not faults; they are character lines. Imagine the tales these lines can tell of the soul. Their stories are why I am drawn to quilts featuring the older generation.

As you begin to work on wrinkles, it is important to etch the grooves using dark tones. In the areas where there are fine lines, I follow the path with a lighter value of thread and create what the viewer will perceive as texture. Over the textured surface I use a lighter thread. The slightly darker color below will blend in once the lighter thread is added. This can be seen on Judy's nose and below her lips. It is important to approach this texture in an almost tentative manner. Too much color underlying the finish threads will create a mottled appearance. Being subtle is the key!

As you begin your journey into the texture of a face, it is important to know that you may use as many as 30 different colors in creating the final image, but you need to concentrate on the dark areas first.

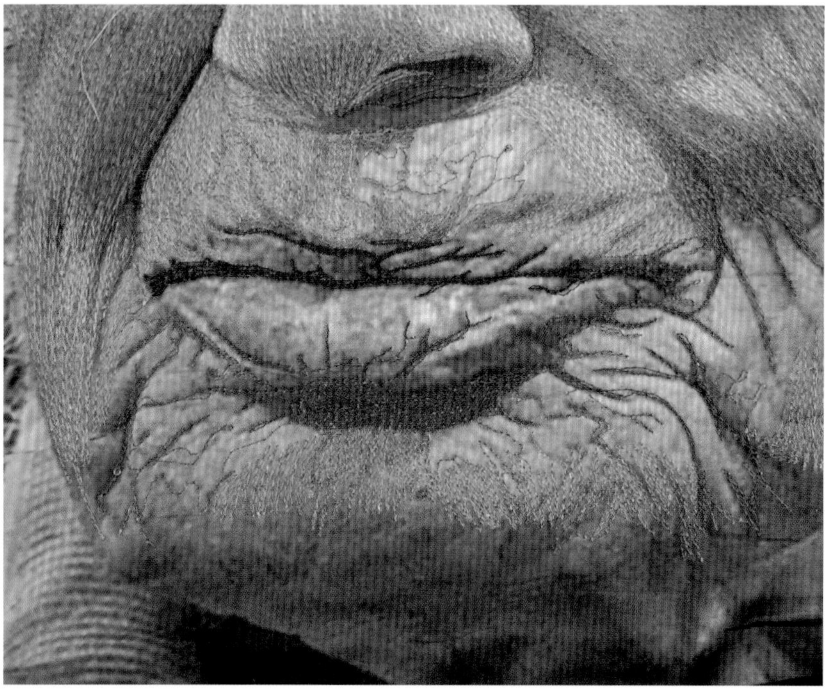

Details from *Judy* (see full quilt, page 110)

Lips

Lips are almost as important as eyes in the perception of the viewer. They can be stern or soft and sensuous. Judy's lips are very textured. I added an underlayer of the darker tone using the sketchy-scratchy technique (page 52). After the topmost threads are applied, the lips are complete. I used six different threads to create the lips.

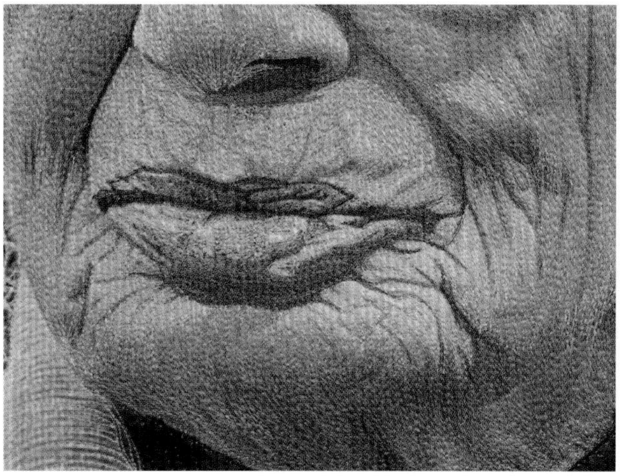

Eyes

Judy's eyes were also a bit of a challenge. I decided to leave the whites alone because the whites are actually almost gray. The addition of thread in this area would have detracted from the glorious green of her irises. I also left the highlights in the iris without thread.

Adding six colors of underlying threads to the wrinkles under Judy's eyes is critical to the success of her portrait.

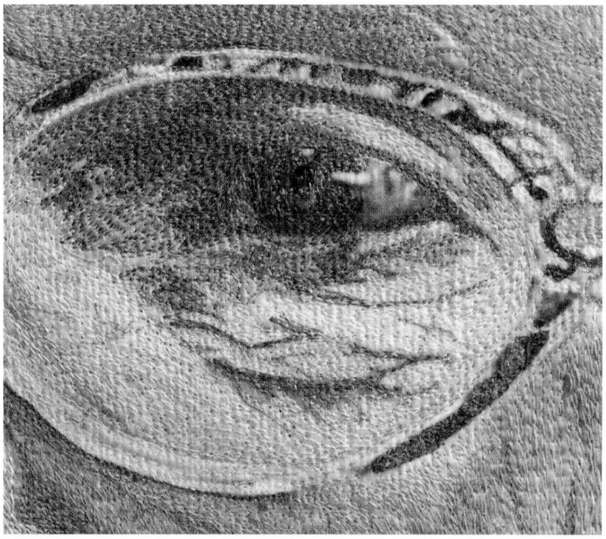

I debated leaving the area behind her glasses without top threads to exaggerate the look of her wearing glasses. Without additional threads within the glasses area, the fabric was puffy and detracted from the overall appearance of the quilt. In the end, I stitched over her wrinkles, and her eyes are portrayed in a more natural state.

CARSON (YOUTHFUL SKIN)

I had almost finished Carson's face when I realized that there was something not quite right. I pulled out the original photograph and displayed it next to the quilt on my design wall. It took a while before I realized there was too much light reflecting on his right cheek.

This is the moment that your true artistic ability will come to the fore. Once you think you are finished, I encourage you to display your work on your design wall and spend a lot of time studying it. Please do not spend hours tackling every detail. That will lead to an overworked piece of art that can easily be destroyed with too much attention.

I decided to change the light along the edge of Carson's cheekbone. To do this, I added a sketchy-scratchy (page 52) bit of thread along the cheek. My goal was to create a shadow instead of an area of bright light along the side of his face.

I then blended the thread from the highlighted area over the edges of the newly added cheek color and achieved my goal. Now, the bridge of the nose and the highest part of the cheekbone contain the light, and the shadow at the bone of the cheek is more pronounced. This is a softer and more realistic approach to his features.

Detail from *Carson and the Barn Cat* (see full quilt, page 109)

As you analyze each portrait, you will see areas of light and dark that may need to be refined. The addition of another thread can unify the features of the individual. When stitched together closely, threads will almost fuse together, tricking the eye into seeing a color that is not really there. **Remember—thread is your paint.**

hair

Wisdom by Jennifer Day, 33″ × 40″, 2010

It is very exciting to begin the process of creating hair using thread painting. Because of the flyaway nature of hair, there is no right or wrong way to do this! You can let your imagination run wild when choosing threads. A brunette can have streaks of gold or red running through her locks. An old man's or woman's head or beard may have twenty shades of gray. You will have a lot of fun creating blonds using all the shades in between honey and platinum. Strands of hair are never straight. They are all over the map with their twists and turns. Hair is texture and color combined. An amazing textural design is created when you add several different tones and colors to hair.

This is the icing on the cake in portraiture. The eyes make the person come alive, and the hair adds excitement and personality to the individual.

Each strand of hair in his beard was a single line of stitching. It is important to let some of the hairs be constructed of solitary stitches to capture the thinness of the hair. The interior portion of his beard was easier. I made swirling motions to create the feel of his grizzled beard. Sewing in a continuous motion is easier than starting and stopping and cutting threads.

The hair on Donald's head is also made with long, continuous lines of stitching. I used twelve colors of white in his beard and hair. The layering of these threads creates texture.

Detail of *Wisdom* (see full quilt, page 59)

DARK HAIR

For the hair, I again start with the darkest thread color first and go from dark to light, but then I will add odd colors to the hair as I finish this part of the project. This gives sheen to the hair, and the individual glows with light.

Leaving space between the individual hairs is good at the beginning of this process. It makes it easier to see where strands of lighter hair occur on the photograph below. These lighter strands are added last. In the following photographs, two more shades of color are added to the dark brown. I begin to allow a strand or two to drift over the areas of dark brown, allowing the lighter tone to take on a life of its own. Lastly, I add a few more dark strands over the others to create a tousled look to this head of hair.

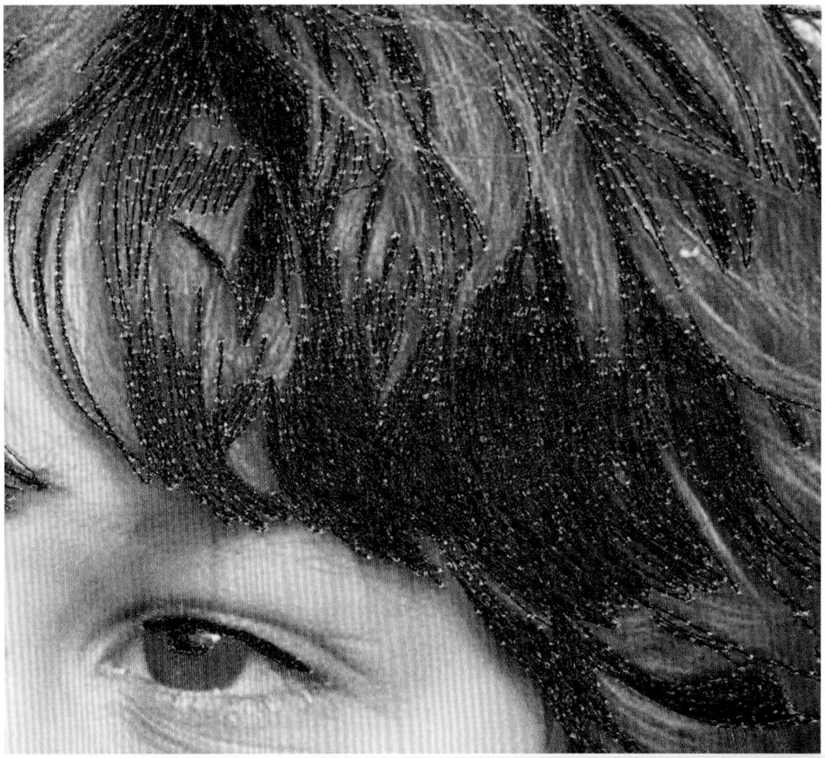

STREAKS OF LIGHT

Alex's hair is done in the same free-form manner as Dark Hair (page 61), but this time I started with the highlights in her hair so I would not lose them as I stitched the darker threads. After the application of the chestnut color, I sewed the dark brown and the gray tones. The gray threads represent light reflecting in her hair. This is almost a posterized effect, but by adding more threads I mute the final product.

The last step is a soft brown thread stitched over the balance of her hair, filling in the areas without thread. I purposely left some areas unstitched—the dark brown area at the back of her head has lines that are created by the absence of thread. I also did not include thread on the darkest portion of her topknot. I wanted the photograph to softly blend with the areas covered in strands of thread. I added a bit of flesh-colored thread at the top of her head where the hair is pulled back in her rubber band. It would have been too distracting to see the color of a rubber band in this photograph, so I eliminated the band completely by twisting threads over it. This gives her a carefree appearance.

The addition of tendrils of hair over the face is what truly brings the portrait to life. Alex's skin tones are pretty, but the contrast of the strands of hair accentuates the softness of her silhouette. The minute you add the texture of hair to a portrait, the face begins to glow with a sense of self. It is important to keep the hairs thin and wispy as they lie across the face. Pay particular attention to the movement of the hair. The contrast of the straight strands near Alex's eyes and the open spiral near her chin accentuates the sense of motion as she swings the spoon toward the spools of thread in the finished quilt (see *Beginnings*, page 47). The addition of the free-motion quilting in the background in a pattern that mimics the movement of her hair adds to the fluidity of this piece of art.

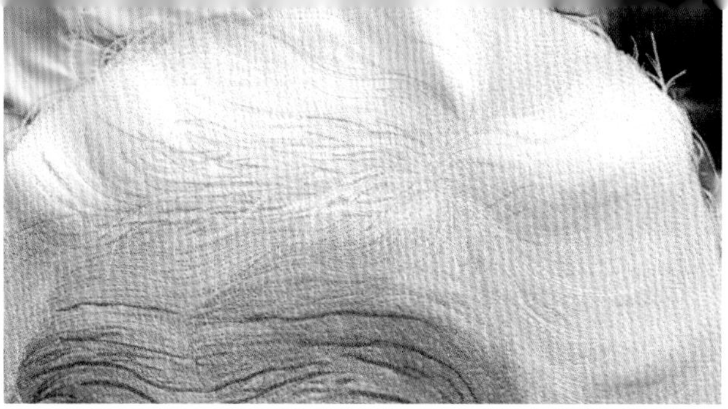

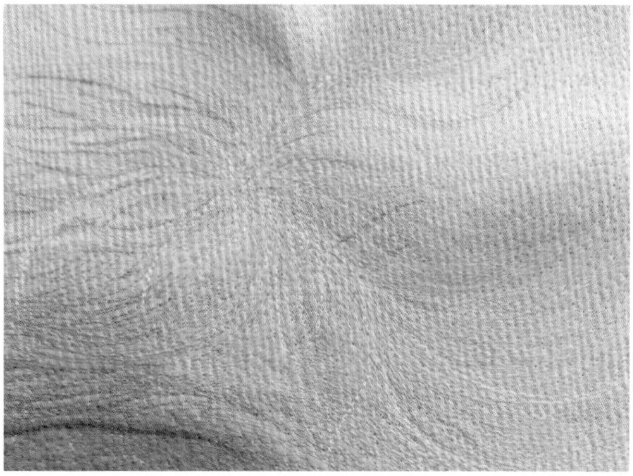

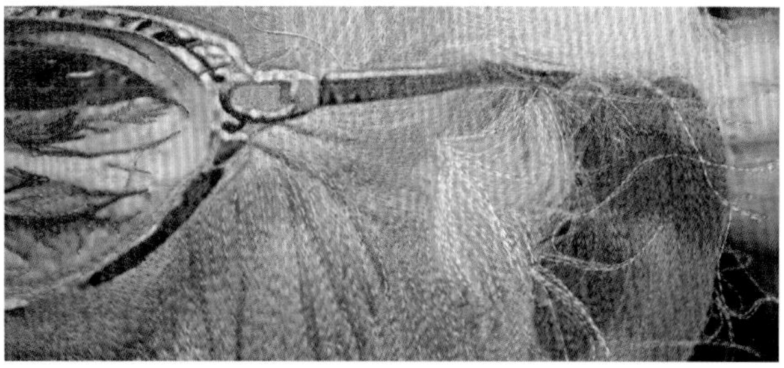

WHITE AND GRAY HAIR

When working with totally white hair it is important to add texture by including shades of gray. This is the only way the viewer will see the soft waves of the hair. Because Judy's hair is totally white, I added only a few streaks of light gray to give her hair movement. I could have added darker streaks without repercussions, since strands of white thread can be added later to blend the tones together (see *Judy*, page 110).

The top of Judy's head is a perfect example of leaving the lines of stitching with space between them and letting the color of the photograph below do part of the work for you. If you decide that the single strand of darker brown near the top of this photograph is too intrusive, more white threads can be twisted over the top to blend the coloration.

Silk, rayon, and embroidery threads are a perfect addition to a quilt to give the hair a shiny patina. I encourage you to mix matte and shiny threads together to give hair drama. By adding just a few strands of silk at Judy's temple, I gave her a totally different look than if the hair here had had only a matte finish. This accentuates her age and brings brightness to her face.

Adding just a touch of gray to a dark head of hair is also an exciting task. In this example, because the foundation is already laid in coils of dark twisted strands, the application of single gray hairs is easy. Let your imagination run wild as you apply the new colors.

Because there is such a contrast in the color of the threads, it is important to pay particular attention to the direction of the hairs at the temples and near the part on the top of the head. These strands frame the face and give definition to the hair. They also will help create contrasting drama as the eye is drawn to the curls that are stitched over the rest of the head.

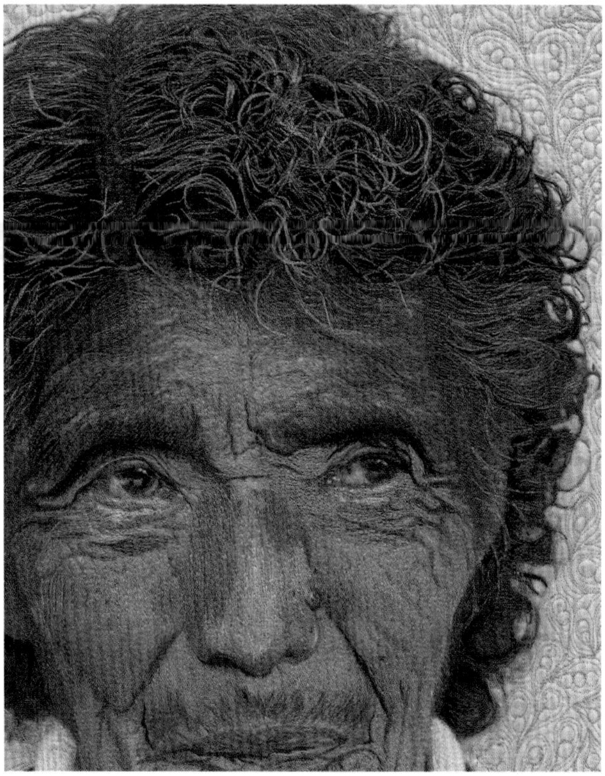

Detail from *Grace* (see full quilt, page 65)

BLONDS

A mass of blond hair is an adventure to stitch in thread. Dakota's head of hair is comprised of 14 different thread colors. I could have finished it with as few as 6 colors, but I was driven to keep adding texture and color to this tousled mop. I started with the dark streaks and then worked my way toward the lighter shades of color. Amazingly, I finished his hair in a total of two hours of nonstop sewing, with 30 changes of thread. I would add color after color, then sit back and realize that I needed a bit more ash blond over the cream that I had just sewn.

Sewing a head of hair is good for relaxation. Your mind gets caught up in the rhythm and the joy of creation. Time disappears, and when you are finished you sit back and smile with a feeling of accomplishment!

Dakota by Jennifer Day, 22″ × 22″, 2014

hands

Grace by Jennifer Day, 39″ × 56″, 2012

Behold the hands, how they promise, conjure, appeal, menace, pray, supplicate, refuse, beckon, interrogate, admire, confess, cringe, instruct, command, mock, and what not besides, with a variation and multiplication of variation which makes the tongue envious.

~ Michel de Montaigne

Thousands of words have been written about hands in literature and poetry. Hands are a symbol of protection, power, and strength. People reach for each other's hands as a sign of rapport, respect, concern, trust, and romance. There are more nerve endings in human hands than in any other part of the body, which renders them the most useful and powerful parts of our body. Leonardo Di Vinci's, Vincent Van Gogh's, and Salvador Dali's works include many paintings and drawings of hands. You must learn how to capture the essence of hand movement in your portraits.

The hand gesture that is portrayed in *Grace* (page 65) tells a book's worth of stories. Angela has drawn her hand to her bosom to rest it there. Her veins are readily visible, and there is bruising over the top of her hand; her finger has a small bandage. Her middle finger is arthritic, but her nails are long and well kept. I took this photograph of Angela as she sat in the Plaza in Santa Fe, New Mexico, selling her pottery. I could not decide whether she was a bit uncomfortable being faced with a long-lens camera or whether she was just deigning to allow me to photograph her on a hot afternoon. Her hand is held with grace, hence the name of the quilt.

ELDERLY HANDS

The direction of stitching is critical to the success of a hand executed in thread. The colors in the photograph are intense. I added only a few lines in the deepest tones to create emphasis. After I stitched these threads, I began to add the texture of the fine lines in the hand over the original threads. My thread painting is lightly spaced over the photograph. This is easily seen along the fingers. I am purposely taking the stitches from left to right with a curve across the bone of the finger to enhance the structure of the woman's fingers.

In order to augment the veins, I added a highlight of cream thread where light is reflected in the crook of her little finger and along the veins in her hand. Allowing the photograph's coloration to be seen through the threads adds texture to the image.

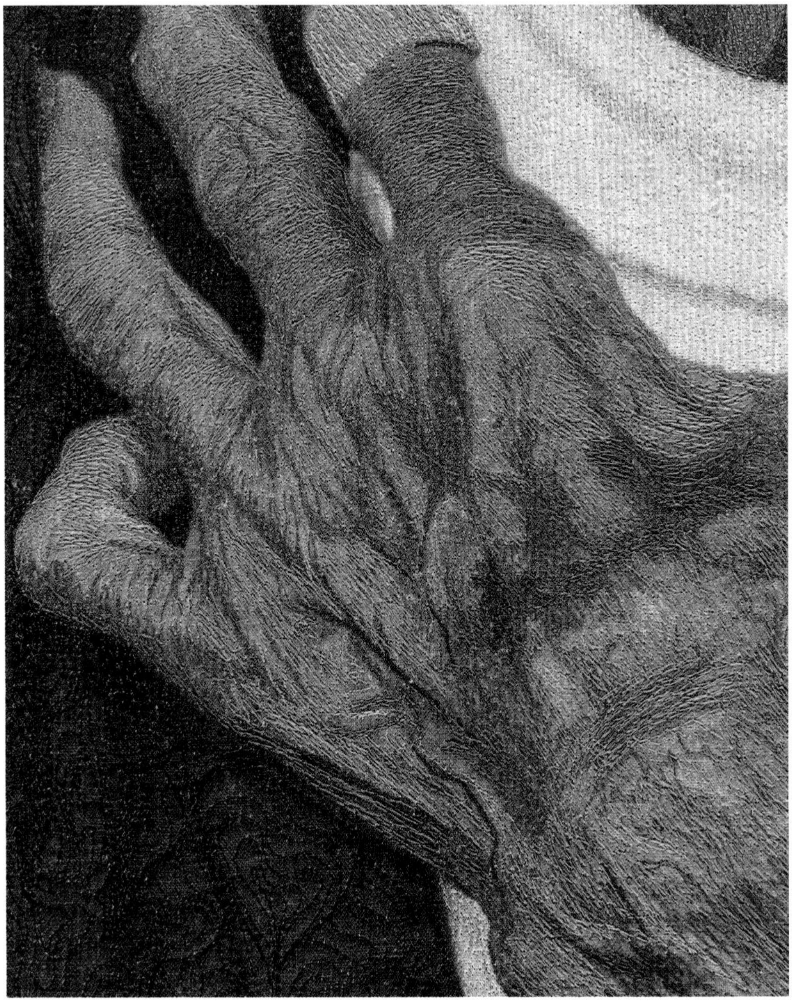

Tibetan Treasure depicts a monk holding a bowl in his hands as he sits cross-legged on the ground. Is the bowl for tea, or is he requesting alms to assist him in his journeys? In this example, I totally covered the photograph with threads. Not seeing any of the original photograph forces the observer to see the portrait as a work of art. I stitched all the threads in this piece in a cohesive pattern from fingertip to knuckle. The only threads that are curved are along the knuckle and represent the folds of the skin. The bottom finger is almost posterized in its appearance, while the threads of the top fingers are well blended.

One of the most interesting details in this quilt is the cracked and dirty fingernails. It was easy to blend the texture of the nail and the dirt together seamlessly.

Detail from *Tibetan Treasure* (see full quilt, page 105)

YOUNG HANDS

Young hands do not have the character of the hands of older people. There are very soft folds to the skin that don't easily register changes in light. The fourteen colors that I used to create the colors of this child's skin need to blend without a wrinkle to distinguish sections of the hand. Having a photograph handy to refer to is important when stitching areas of skin that are smooth and have little deviation in color. My threads covered the photographic image in its entirety, so having the photograph nearby was important because the reference points are quickly lost as thread is applied to the quilt.

There is only a suggestion of the fingernail bed on the fingers directly below the butterfly. I was drawn to this image because of the dirt under the child's nails. He was playing in the dirt in a garden when the butterfly came to rest on his chubby fingers. This adds to the air of mystery surrounding this piece. I chose to finish the arm of the child in free-motion quilting. This allowed the emphasis in the quilt to be completely on the hands and the butterfly.

Detail from *Garden Wonder* (see full quilt, page 107)

The young man in the quilt details at right is drinking water from a mountain stream in Colorado. As this was one of my early quilts, I used the posterization technique (page 25) to prepare the image. An image that is posterized loses its detail—darker threads between the fingers separate them only slightly, and the knuckles on the fingers are lost. I am sure the only reason this boy's fingernails are not dirty is that he had been playing in the cold mountain steam's water!

Details from *Hot Day, Cool Water* (see full quilt, page 104)

clothing

Dance to the Music by Jennifer Day, 43″ × 34″, 2014

Dance to the Music portrays a young flamenco dancer performing on the bandstand on the Plaza in Santa Fe, New Mexico. Her clothing is a vital part of the story being told. The swirl of her huge skirt in its magnificent colors is mesmerizing. The joy she expresses as she dances to the music is beautiful to behold. I used 84 colors of thread in the quilt and used free-motion quilting on her skirt to mimic and enhance the movement of the swirling cloth.

For every Thread Stories quilt you make, you need to decide how important the clothing is and how much attention you want to focus on it. The options are as follows:

- Use free-motion quilting
- Continue thread painting and cover all the clothing with thread
- Construct appliqués using many different fabrics
- Any combination of the above

USING FREE-MOTION QUILTING

The majority of my quilts incorporate free-motion quilting in the clothing. I enjoy the process of selecting a quilting pattern that reflects the personality of the person wearing the clothes.

Larry, wearing an elegant pinstripe shirt, repairs my sewing machines in Santa Fe, New Mexico. I chose to accentuate the pinstripes on his shirt by stitching them in a slightly contrasting color. Larry's dapper attire is integral to the storyline of this quilt. He always dresses very well as he repairs our machines.

Detail from *Larry* (see full quilt, page 34)

For *Grace*, I used a lotus flower design on the old woman's clothing; it maintains a graceful movement but is not intricate. In this quilt, the attention of the viewer is drawn to the woman.

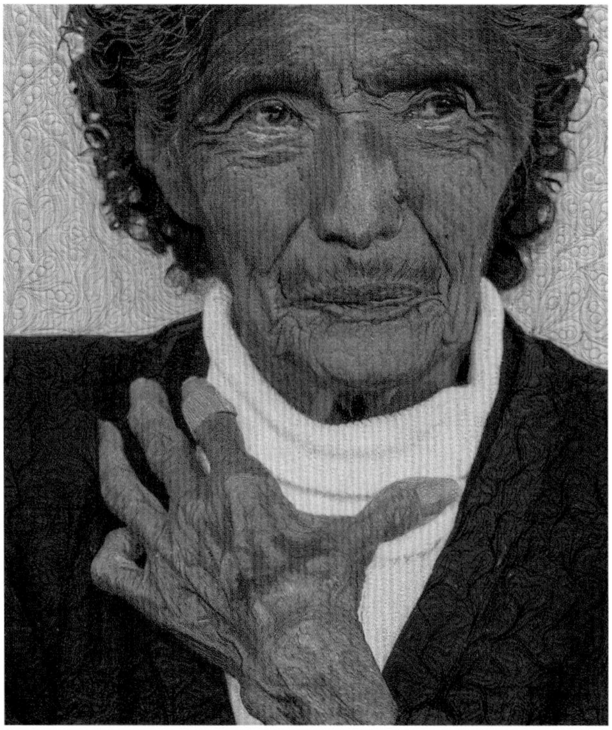

Detail from *Grace* (see full quilt, page 65)

For *Mmm...Good*, I chose a free-flowing quilting design for the child's top. The flowered portion of her shirt was enhanced with free-motion pebbles, paisleys, and hearts. The goal was to create sweetness in the design that reflected the girl's personality.

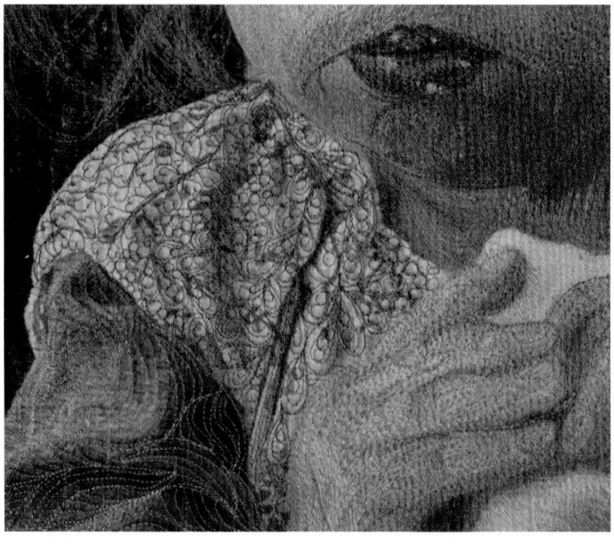

Detail from *Mmm...Good* (see full quilt, page 107)

CLOTHING COVERED IN THREAD

In *Butterflies Are Free*, the swirling diaphanous gown sets the tone for a woman who is at peace and is as free as the butterflies at her fingertips. Her floating image makes us breathe deeply and wish we could join her. Her image is completely thread painted with 92 different colors of thread. The background is a montage of free-motion quilting enhancing her movement. I chose to cover all of her gown in thread and leave the free-motion quilting in the background. The reason for this is that I wanted the viewer's eye to be drawn to the woman's entire body without the distraction of thread movement in her clothing.

Detail from *Butterflies Are Free* (see full quilt, page 21)

In *Holy Cow*, I chose to cover the boys' pants entirely in thread. This is an early quilt of mine that used the posterization process on the photograph (see Posterization, page 25). Because they are boys, I felt that free-motion quilting on their clothing would not project the appropriate texture of boys' wear.

Detail from *Holy Cow* (see full quilt, page 105)

APPLIQUÉ

As mentioned earlier (see Canvas, page 11), you can deliberately choose to stitch on a duplicate printed image using lightweight canvas, which will result in ripples, as seen in Abuela's dress (below). This rippled fabric can then be appliquéd onto your work and incorporated into the overall piece. This technique would also be a good way to add texture to flowers or other subjects.

Detail from *Abuela* (see full quilt, page 101)

COMBINATION

In *Cooking with the Sun*, the light captures the ripples of the woman's skirt in the sun. I chose to highlight these areas by capturing the light in free-motion pebbles, mimicking the blue dots on her skirt. There were 402 blue dots that I covered in thread. What a job, but it was worth it! I left the parts of her skirt in shadow without any stitching at all. Because there were unstitched spaces between the dots, the fabric has lift that mirrors the movement of the skirt in the hot desert wind.

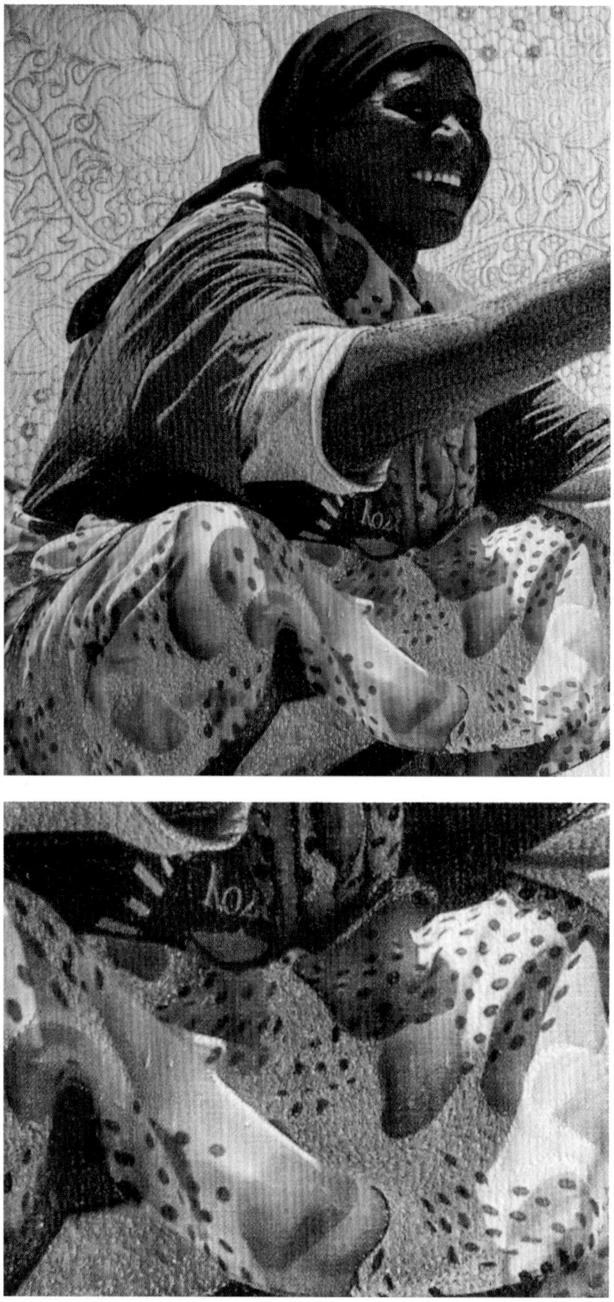

Details from *Cooking with the Sun* (see full quilt, page 106)

pet portraits

It's Raining Cats and Dogs by Jennifer Day, 41″ × 37″, 2014

Pet photography is not easy. Dogs may come when you call (or not), and cats may mysteriously appear at the sound of a can opener, but point a camera at them and they suddenly develop a mind of their own. Cats' typical reaction may be to come right up to the camera in curiosity or turn their tail toward the camera. Dogs will almost automatically turn their back to the camera in a motion of disgust at being photographed. Throw into the mix the challenge of focusing and adjusting the exposure, and we have a cocktail of complexity that makes getting a great pet photograph a real challenge.

We all love our pets. Many times they are better friends than our spouses or children. We love having their pictures near us. Taking their picture is not always easy, though. They do not understand us and won't pose for the camera on command. Here are some thoughts that will help you help you get the most out of your pet's photo session.

TAKING THE PERFECT PET PORTRAIT

Use Natural Light

Use natural light whenever possible; using a flash will cause red-eye and probably frighten the animal. If you are photographing an animal with very dark or black fur, the dark hairs tend to absorb light, so try to slightly overexpose your images. Go outside or, if that is not possible, use a room that is well lit by a large window.

Focus on the Eyes

As with people, the eyes are the window to the soul, and your pet's eyes can be very expressive. Get his attention so he is looking directly at you when you snap the photograph. Try a toy that contains a squeak or a bell, or use something else you know attracts his attention.

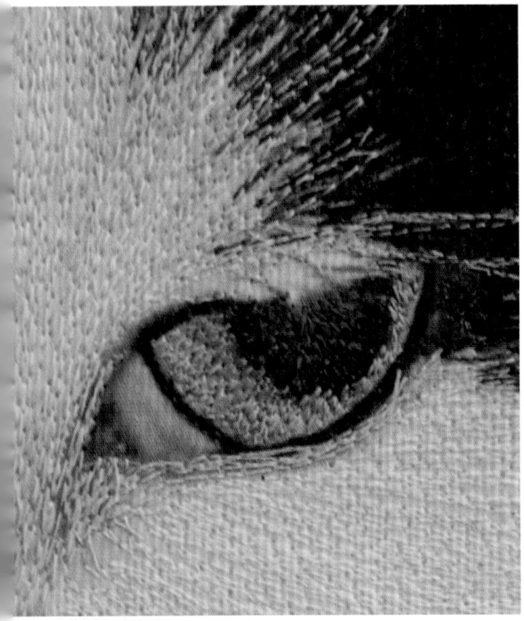

Detail from *Lily* (see full quilt, page 96)

Surprise Them

One of the most difficult things is to capture your pet sitting still. An easy trick is to let him play quietly. When you have everything ready, let someone call for him or whistle or shake a toy that contains a squeak or a bell. This will surprise him and catch his attention. You will then have a few seconds to capture your pet in a nice and alert pose.

Go to Them

It is very important that your pet feels comfortable and at ease—instead of forcing him to come to you, go to him. Get down on his level. We all know how animals look when viewed from above; this is the way we always see them. To create perfect memories, capture them as they see the world. Sit on the floor or lie on your belly and remember to shoot from their eye level.

Give Value to Their Character

You know your pet better than anyone else, and a successful picture is one that conveys the character of its subject. If you have a lazy cat, show him yawning. If your animal is playful, show him in action performing his favorite trick. The goal is to capture your pet's personality.

Think about Context

Your choice of location for the perfect pet shot depends on where your pet is feels at ease and comfortable. Find a location that will evoke memories and emotions for you as the pet's owner in years to come. For example, you might have a place where you and your pet have shared some special moments together, a place that will mean a lot in the future as you view your artwork. Consider the background of your shots carefully. Ultimately, you don't want the background to distract from the photo—sometimes the best locations are the plainest ones, such as a large patch of green grass, a well-lit room with white walls, or a favorite blanket.

Go Macro

Put on that long camera lens and fill the frame with your pet's face and fur; close-up shots often make beautiful animal portraits.

Be Patient

Pet photography requires a lot of patience. No matter how excited your furry friend is, if you are patient enough he will relax and you will have the opportunity capture a priceless memory.

EYES

Again, the eyes are the first part of the quilt to stitch when creating a portrait of your pet. It is critical to capture the look in your best friend's eyes.

The cat's eye in the photo at right is a fabulous green. I stitched it in a circular motion using two colors of green to enhance the brilliance of the iris. I left the black of the pupil and the highlights without thread. Sometimes stitching the pupil will "muddy the water" with thread that takes the attention away from the intense color of the iris.

The dog's eye below right was stitched in the same circular motion, but I used only one color in the iris. A slightly lighter thread color on the fur nearest the eye gives dimension to the eye. Subtle changes in shading are important to the finished product. There are three more shades of color blended together under the dog's eye.

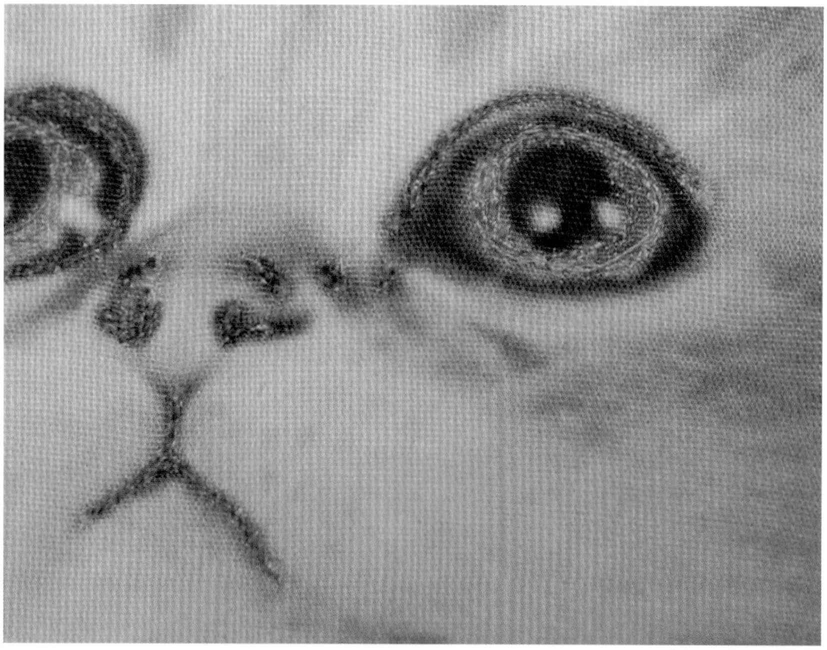

Details from It's Raining Cats and Dogs (see full quilt, page 73)

MOUTH

Every animal's mouth tells a different story. Strong jaws, teeth that can bite, and soft creases in fur are all different from animal to animal in their appearance. Try to pick the moment for your photograph that tells the story of your friend. Images of a cat licking her fur or a dog's mouth open in excitement are what you want to catch with your photography. My dog Rain has her mouth open with surprise as she watches bubbles floating through the air.

Capturing her open mouth with all the colors involved was an interesting challenge. I started with the darkest color first and extended it past the mouth to the fur on her head. Then I worked my way from the darkest to the lightest of the brown tones inside her mouth. The next step was to blend the colors in her lips with the tones of her tongue. I successfully used ten colors of thread in this small space of the quilt. It is amazing how our pets smile at us every day. It is our mission to catch these magic moments in our art.

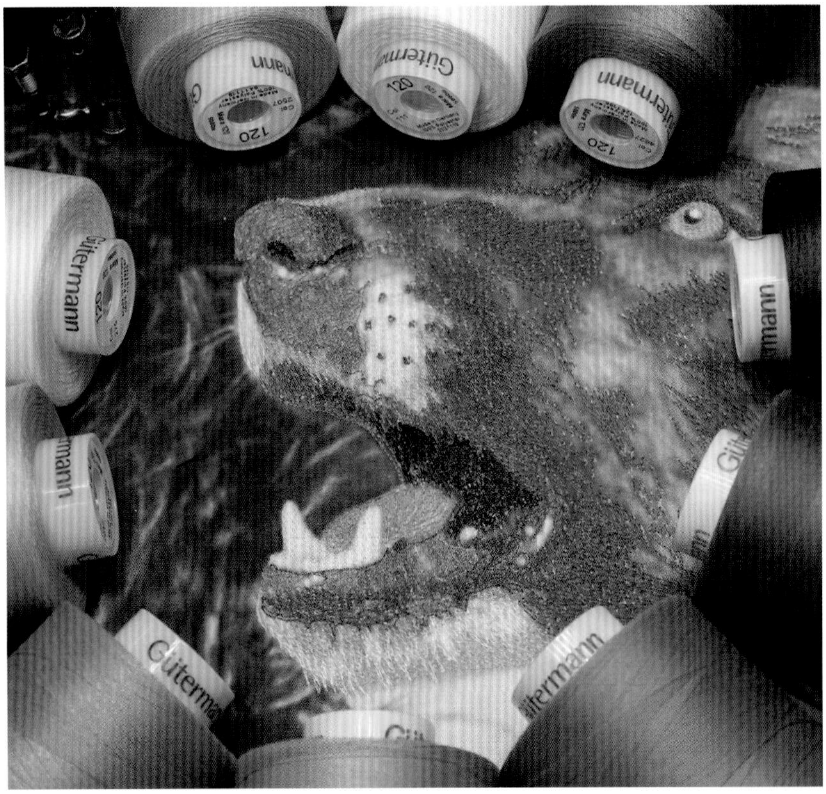

Detail from *It's Raining Cats and Dogs* (see full quilt, page 73)

FUR

Fur is treated exactly the same as human hair in the stitching process (see Hair, page 59).

Fur, like hair, is a study in texture that adds interest to the portrait. The composition of individual hairs lends character to the animal. Every pet has a few tufts of fur that always lie in the same direction that are a distinguishing characteristic. If you can capture a few of these, then you will look at your artwork and smile! The goal is to highlight the colorations in the fur by blending several different colors in a small space.

The leg of B Bear, my Old English sheepdog, is a perfect study in texture (page 77). I started with the darkest of the five colors in the shadows of his leg. Single lines of stitching emphasize where the fur is ruffled and allow the viewer to perceive the coarseness of the hairs that are clumped together.

After all the threads are blended together, the fur takes on a life of its own. By leaving space between the threads on the paws, you allow the observer's eye to pick up the individual stitches, and this also creates texture in the hairs. It is important to blend the shadows very gradually up the leg so that the white hairs capture the light.

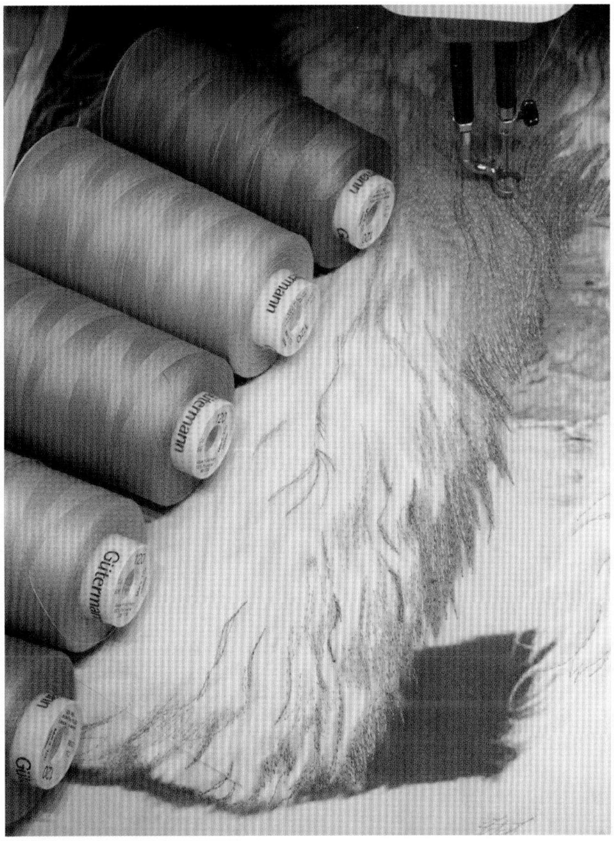

Details from *It's Raining Cats and Dogs* (see full quilt, page 73)

I have followed the same technical steps on the cat, starting with the darkest thread and working to the lightest.

The cat's face was finished with the cream-colored threads spaced slightly apart to allow the photograph to show from underneath. This allows the individual stitches to be seen, and the texture of the stitching comes to the fore.

Details from *It's Raining Cats and Dogs* (see full quilt, page 73)

WHISKERS

How Are Whiskers Different from Other Hair?

When it comes to pet hair, whiskers are longer, thicker, and more rigid, as well as more deeply embedded in the skin. Each whisker is rooted in a hair follicle that is filled with blood vessels and nerves.

Most cats have twelve whiskers on either cheek, arranged in four rows, but the whisker pattern in dogs is more varied. Whiskers can also sprout above the eyes, as well as under the chin. Cats can also grow whiskers behind their wrists.

When you are creating a pet portrait, the dark hairs where the whiskers originate need to be stitched first. The cat's 24-plus whiskers will result in 24-plus cuts of thread unless you try the following technique: Start in one area, laying down multiple threads, and then move the needle to the next spot. Leave a long thread between the starting and stopping points so that the threads are easier to snip when you are finished sewing. This takes only a few minutes to execute.

After the threads are snipped, you have a perfect place to begin stitching the white whiskers from. Be careful that you do not cover all the dark threads with the white whiskers.

Details from *Carson and the Barn Cat* (see full quilt, page 109)

BIRDS

Chicken Vermeer by Jennifer Day, 22″ × 18″, 2012

Detail from *Chicken Vermeer*

Birds are very interesting to stitch, and following the angle of the feathers is natural. Birds have hundreds of colors in their plumage, and picking colors from dark to light is the first step. Minding the minute gradations between the tones is important to allow the feathers to blend together seamlessly. Oftentimes I will add silk, rayon, or embroidery threads to a bird portrait to create a sheen on the feathers.

Notice that I have left space between the threads on *Chicken Vermeer*. The space adds another facet to the quilt and is perceived as texture by the viewer. Like hair or fur on a dog or cat, texture is indispensible in conveying realism in birds.

Parrot by Jennifer Day, 31″ × 22″, 2015; based on an original photo by Guido Daniele

The quilt *Parrot* is an amazing combination of matte polyester, rayon, and silk threads. The sheen of the rayon and silk imitate the way light strikes a bird's feathers, making them glow with rich color. This quilt has 94 different colors of thread in it. The blending of colors together is seamless due to the number of threads used and the minute graduation of colors.

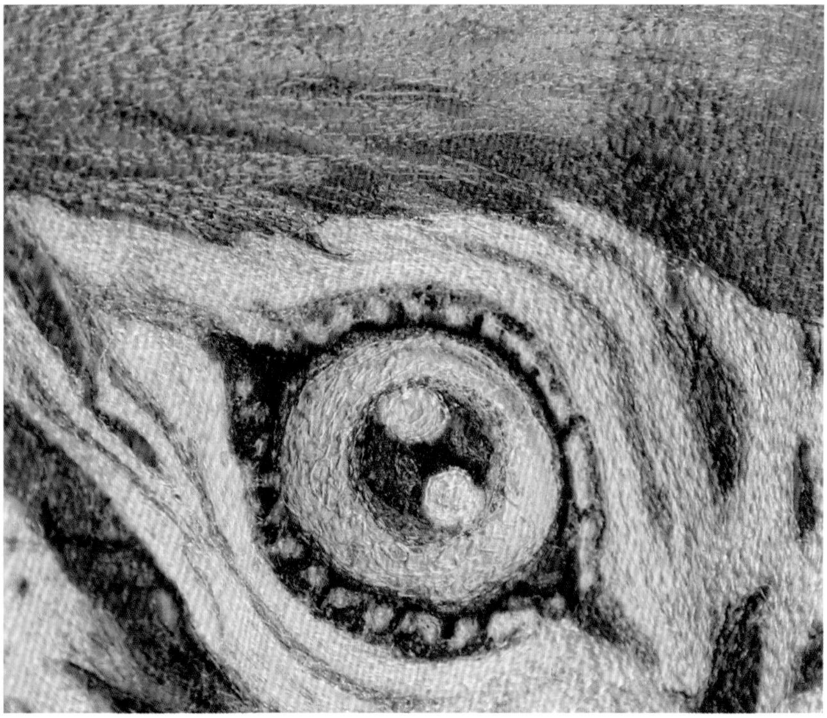

Detail of *Parrot*

free-motion quilting

Memories by Jennifer Day, 31″ × 45″, 2013

As with all quilts, Thread Stories quilts are held together with quilting. I prefer free-motion quilting for the background, using designs that enhance the central image of the quilt and help tell the story. Occasionally I also use free-motion stitching on the clothing of the subject as well. The goal is to allow the free-motioned areas to recede and the thread-painted portions of the artwork to come to the fore.

There are many resources for free-motion quilting designs (see Resources, page 111). Sometimes I'm inspired by a design from a book or the Internet, and other times I use these resources as a starting point and spin off my own designs.

CHOOSING A FREE-MOTION DESIGN

Many times choosing a pattern is mind-boggling; with so many curves, curls, dips, and lines to choose from, it is hard to decide what pattern will provide the best glimpse of the personality of the subject of your quilt.

I like using paisleys, florals, and soft curves for the elderly. There is an elegance and sophistication in older women that demands a refined approach. For example, in *Memories*, a 96-year-old woman is sitting in her doorway in Havana, Cuba, on a Sunday afternoon waiting for her family to arrive. She is dressed in her nightclothes covered with pink flowers and a warm sweater. A pink towel is draped across her lap and a tissue rests on it. I chose a graceful free-motion quilting design for her sweater that lends an air of elegance to her persona. I also enhanced the flowers on her nightgown with several colors of thread. The background is a soft floral pattern that contrasts with the straighter lines of her hair.

Detail from *Memories* (see full quilt, page 81)

Beginnings has the same lotus flower and paisley patterns that were used in the background of *Memories*. In *Beginnings*, the designs appear sweet and innocent.

Detail from *Beginnings* (see full quilt, page 47)

For *Baby in Hand*, I chose a repetitive pattern of waves. I used a simple background because I wanted all the attention on the newborn. I did incorporate dark circles of thread to add some interest. The backdrop almost makes it look as though the baby is floating in space and reaching out to the unknown on her first day on earth.

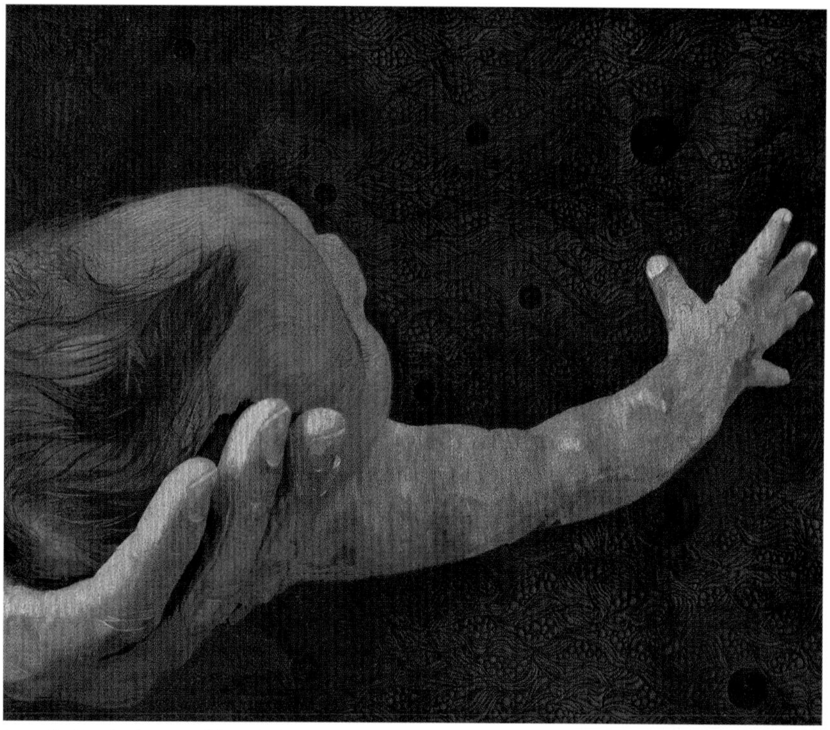

Detail of *Baby in Hand* (see full quilt, page 103)

The quilt on the wall in *Larry* presented opportunities for free-motion quilting that are not available on a blank canvas. I chose to enhance the patterns on the quilt background with threads that duplicate the lines, with some twists and turns to augment the appearance of each block.

Detail from *Larry* (see full quilt, page 34)

Abuela features a woman sitting in an open window of an old adobe building in New Mexico. I purposely chose to leave a portion of the adobe wall without stitching so that it visually comes to the fore, drawing attention to the decaying plaster over the adobe bricks. The intense stitching along the top of the adobe bricks highlights this area. The ripple of the unstitched cloth duplicates the rough texture of the plaster. The unstitched area enhances the thread painting on the woman's face.

Because the central image of a Thread Stories quilt is thread painted and the threads are stitched on top of each other, it is important that all the other stitching on the quilt be close together so the quilt will lie flat. The free-motion quilting lines should be about ¼″ apart. If the stitching is ½″–1″ (or more) apart, the quilt may appear rippled as the fabric buckles.

Continuous-line free-motion quilting is a perfect way to finish your works of art.

Detail from *Abuela* (see full quilt, page 101)

correcting mistakes

DON'T BE TOO HARD ON YOURSELF

Many times in the life of a quiltmaker, things do not go as planned. Often designs are changed midstream or the technique used is not as smooth in its presentation as you had hoped. This chapter focuses on ways to correct some of the problems you may encounter. I make mistakes too!

Friends by Jennifer Day, 34″ × 45″, 2011

USING APPLIQUÉ

The quilt *Friends* (page 85) is based on a photograph of my son and his best friend walking along a fence line on hot summer day at our ranch in New Mexico. I thread painted both of the boys using a posterized image (see Posterization, page 25).

Unfortunately, the tall dark-haired child, my son, began to look a bit like an alien. The only choice I had to correct the problem was to reprint his head on fabric and appliqué the new head over the top of the original. I added a piece of canvas to the back of the new fabric for stabilization and appliquéd the new head onto the quilt.

In appliquéing this newly stitched image over the first, I needed to smooth the stitching at the arm so there wouldn't be a crease in the spot where the appliqué was placed. I did not want a seam that would readily indicate to the viewer that an appliqué is on the quilt. This is the beauty of painting with thread. Thread covers a multitude of sins.

The end result is a new head on my child and a banished alien!

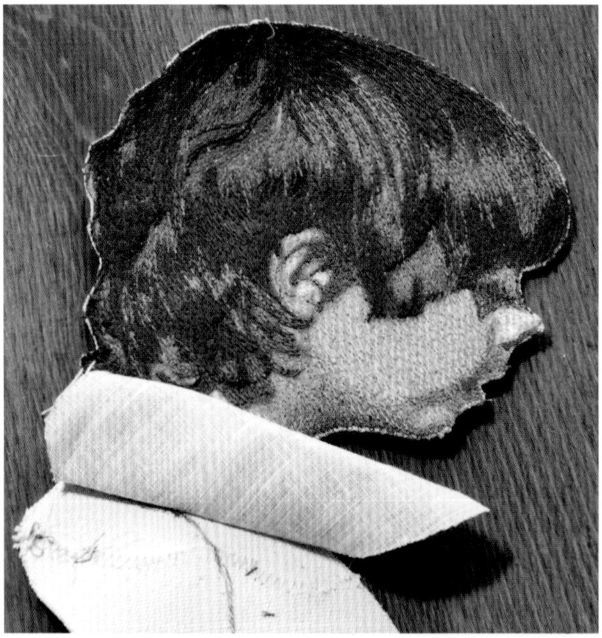

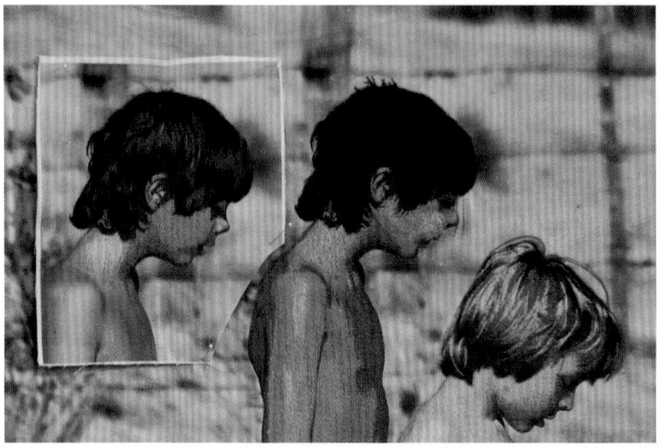

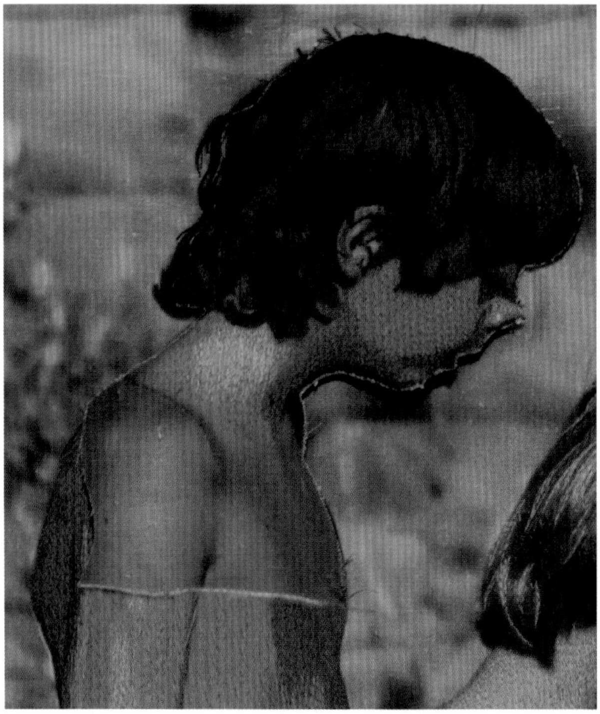

CUTTING TO REMOVE BUBBLES

Sometimes the fabric that is being stitched becomes distorted. This can happen for a variety of reasons. I like to work on a portrait in a radiating format away from the eyes. On *Elisha*, I skipped over the woman's mouth and continued stitching the flesh below her lips. Unfortunately, this created a bubble in the area of her lips and teeth. This is a raised area of fabric that cannot be flattened because of the intense stitching surrounding the bump.

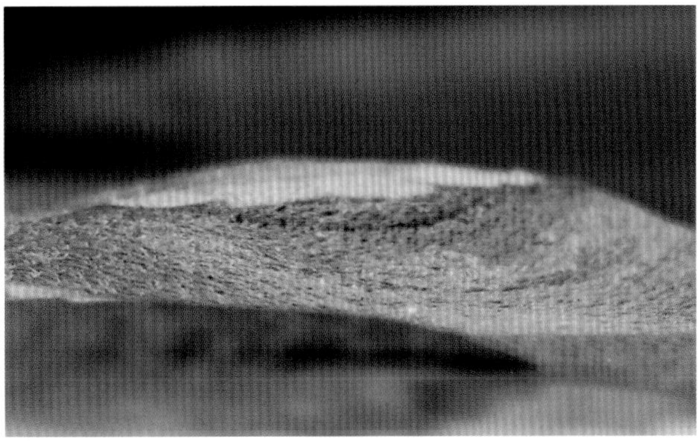

If a sharp blade is used to cut the problem area, releasing the fabric tension, the problem can be solved. A small portion of the fabric needs to be removed with scissors so that when the edges are pressed together the fabric lies flat. It is important to follow a contour on the face that can be restitched with a contrasting thread to disguise the correction. In this photograph, Elisha's face was cut above the lip and along the curve of the nose.

The cut area was restitched with the lip color and the dark color in the crease of the nostril. The fabric now lies flat.

Unfortunately, if slicing and repositioning the fabric does not solve the distortion issue, the only way to fix the problem is to remove a portion of the fabric and appliqué another image over the top of the problem area, as I did in the quilt *Friends* (page 85).

Other distortions can occur when too much thread is stitched in one area. This can cause a recess in the fabric. The only way to correct this problem is to clip some of the threads on the back of the quilt and remove most of them, allowing the fabric to lie flat again.

COVERING OVER WHITE DOTS

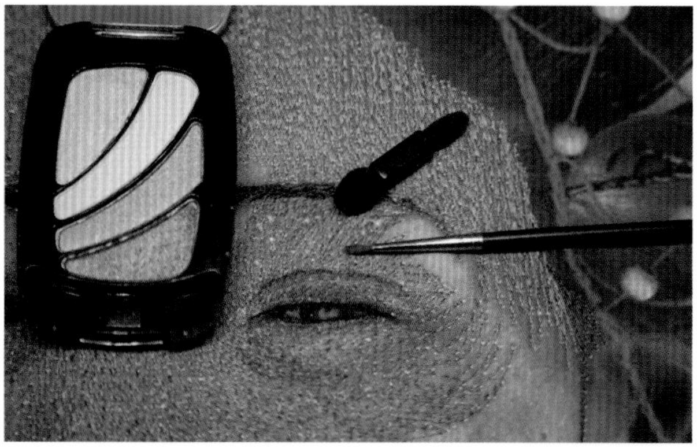

Many times when you are intensely thread painting a quilt, some of the ink that has been printed on the fabric will flake off, leaving a white dot.

Note: The ink is applied to the fabric as a top treatment. Some of the ink will saturate the fabric, but some of the ink when dried can become less stable and flake.

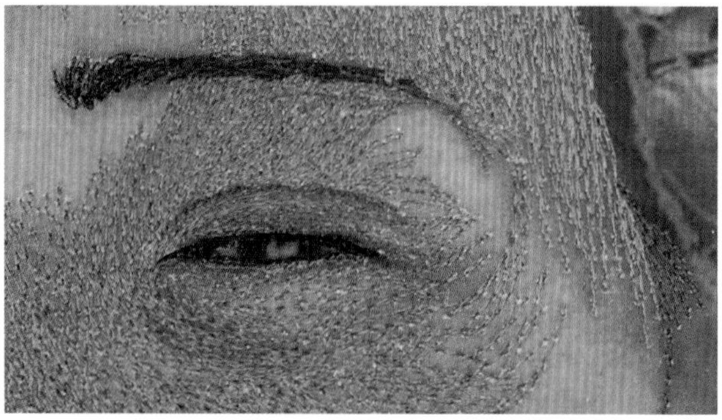

These white dots can easily be stitched over to disguise them, but if the goal is to lightly thread paint an area another solution needs to be explored.

A simple solution is to purchase inexpensive makeup—eye shadow or face powder works best. Select a product with a matte finish; you don't want a sheen or sparkle. Using a brush, gently stroke the shadow over the areas that have the pesky white dots. The makeup will flow into the threads, giving a nice cohesive finish to the area.

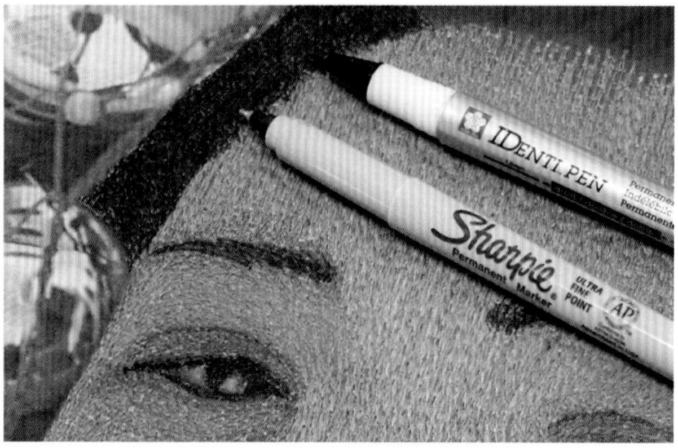

The white dots are most visible when dark threads are used. In this case, a black permanent marker such as an IDenti-pen or Sharpie will easily cover the white dots.

When you are treating these dots, hang the quilt on a wall, stand back, and make a decision about how this quilt is likely to be displayed. Then you can decide whether it's worth spending time correcting this visual issue.

DEALING WITH NEEDLE DEFLECTION

One of the biggest problems my students face in the beginning is needle deflection (when the needle turns or bends), resulting in multiple threads being pulled up to the top of the quilt.

On my domestic machine, I usually use a size 14 needle, but while you are learning the rhythm necessary to move your fabric in sync with the speed of your machine, it may be best to use a size 18 needle or a size 14 titanium-coated top-stitch needle such as those from Superior Threads. Titanium-coated needles are stronger and last longer than regular needles.

I have had days when I continually deflect the needle. On these days it is best to walk away from the machine for a while because your body is out of sync with your desire to quilt. A fresh start usually corrects the problem!

on the flip side

The back of a thread-painted art quilt is almost as fabulous as the front. There are endless possibilities to be explored using the back of a quilt covered in thread.

The inverted image is a much more detailed representation of the photograph. Because the threads are on a blank canvas, the colors of the photograph are not displayed. This allows each and every line of intense stitching to be seen clearly. Mistakes can also be more easily seen. When I first started using this technique, I would constantly check the back of my quilt. Because I could see every stitch, I found myself being more careful with stitch placement on the front of the quilt. Being aware of every stitch has forced me to become a better quilter. Now the backs of my quilts are as clean as the fronts. Every thread is clipped. I remove all areas of poorly adjusted tension, and those annoying balls and tufts of thread are eliminated. I am sure that this degree of cleanup has contributed to my success as I enter juried shows.

Following are just two examples of the reverse of a quilt.

One option is to stitch using bobbin threads that match the threads on the front of the quilt. *Los Mambesis* was created using matching bobbin threads. The result is an almost spooky rendition of the old man. It is also easy to see the hours of work that you have spent creating your art.

Reverse of *Los Mombesis* (see full quilt, page 40)

Reverse of *Judy* (see full quilt, page 101)

I specifically chose the threads pictured for the back of *Judy* to demonstrate how the woman's spirit comes alive. I selected a soft gray tone for the inside of her glasses to accentuate the wrinkles below her eyes. This tells a different story than the image on the front of the quilt. This is what she would have looked like as a much younger woman.

guest fiber artists

More and more artists are being drawn to the world of thread painting. The following pages include quilts that have been created by fellow artists using threads as the main staple in their art. Enjoy!

Abby by Barbara McKie, 15″ × 14″, 2012, based on an original photo by Maria Catalano

Maria Catalano, a visitor to the Somers, New York, quilt show where I had been invited to do a special exhibit, saw my work and asked me to make two quilts of her two recently passed cats, Abby and Lucy. Maria provided the images, but I enhanced them, changed the backgrounds in Photoshop, and then printed them on polyester crepe fabric. I then thread painted and free-motion quilted the cats.

There are two elements involved in *Embracing the Silver Years*: a digital photograph in the background enhanced by quilting, and an appliquéd thread-painted foreground that is heavily padded and "sculpted" to create a strong relief effect. I use a photographic base as a rough guide for the thread painting, but the process is by no means "paint by number." In my mind, my sewing machine becomes a colored pencil with which I blend and enrich colors, much the same as pointillist painters, by placing two colors next to each other to fool the eye into seeing a third color.

The direction of the lines helps define shapes and often creates some warping, even when a strong stabilizer is used. Pockets evolve that can later be stuffed and molded with small hand stitches to produce a sculptural effect. This results in a very uneven weight distribution, so most of my works are mounted on stretcher strips and framed. This piece is an exception.

Embracing the Silver Years by Jayne Bentley Gaskins, 32″ × 46″, 2014

This quilt honors a mature woman, still on life's journey, who has the courage to throw off stereotypes of the past and plot her own course.

Detail of *Embracing the Silver Years*

Photo by Ken Sanville

Panning for Gold
by Lea McComas
31″ × 39″, 2014
This quilt was inspired by a historical photo from the archive of the History Colorado Center, Denver, Colorado.

My work is representational and seeks to recreate and reflect some significant essence of life events. I limit my medium almost exclusively to cloth and thread and combine fiber techniques with principles of classical portrait painting. Using cloth and thread with precision and clarity to create a visual image that touches a memory or emotion buried in the psyche, forcing it to the conscious surface for fresh analysis, is my goal as an artist.

Inspired by a historical photo of a gold miner working a stream, *Panning for Gold* depicts the grit and spirit of those who settled the West. This piece began with a fused fabric base and was covered with stitching to create a lifelike rendering of the prospector. In contrast, the fabric layers and stitching in the background are more obscure and simply hint at the scenery beyond.

Maximum Cat Nap
by Susan Brubaker Knapp
22″ × 18½″, 2010

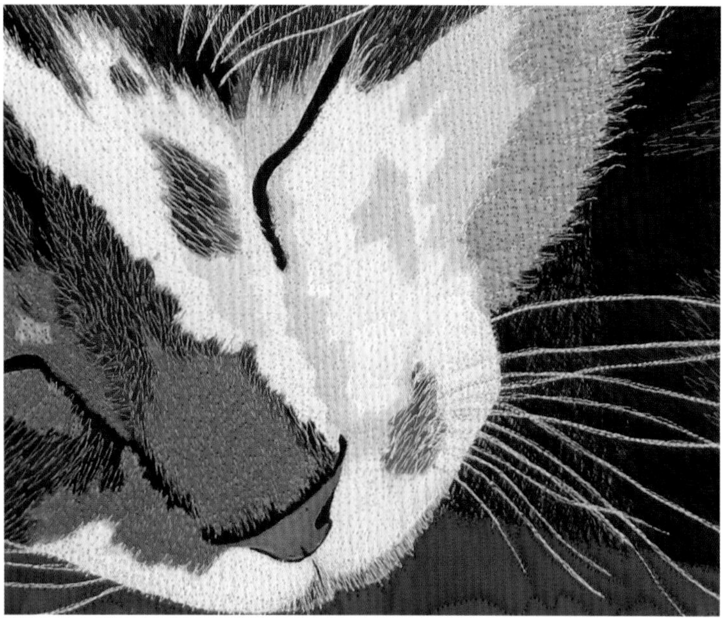

This piece is based on a photo I took of our beloved family cat, Max. I first painted him onto white cotton prepared-for-dyeing fabric, then added interfacing as a stabilizer under the painted fabric, and then heavily thread sketched the piece. I call what I do with thread on the surface of the piece thread sketching because it is lighter than thread painting, allowing the painted surface or the fabric of my fusible appliqué pieces to show through.

To create the look of Max's fur, which often had several shades on each hair, I used lighter thread values on top of darker paint colors. By paying close attention to the direction and coarseness of the different kinds of fur on Max's coat, I created realistic fur. I discovered that Max (like most cats, I now realize) has lots of cowlicks! Only one part of Max's body was left without thread sketching: his smooth nose.

student work

Student work in progress

I love teaching. It always amazes me that after the first day of class, my students "get it." The following quilts were created by my students in my intensive five-day class, taught in Santa Fe, New Mexico. None of these students had any experience with thread painting before arriving for class. By the end of the week, their understanding of how to blend threads to create realistic image of art was firmly established. I am looking forward to seeing more of their work in years to come!

B Bear
by Mary Zahner
8″ × 12″, 2014

This was the thread painting I did the very first day of Jennifer's class in Santa Fe. It is of her dog, B Bear. I finished it in one day. Having quilted for many years, I was thrilled to learn this new approach to art quilting. Helpful advice from Jennifer was to start with the eyes, which are the soul of the picture. From there I sewed the dark areas of the fur. I continued blending and layering thread, as well as putting in some movement to indicate the different directions of the fur. After finishing the face, I did stippling around him. I love the end result!

Lily
by Mary Zahner
18⅛″ × 17″, 2014

I completed the thread painting of my cat, Lily, in Jennifer's five-day class in Santa Fe. I started with eyes. Then I sewed the dark areas of Lily's fur and the shadows that delineate her legs. I blended and layered various colors of white and cream for her fur. This portrait perfectly captures Lily!

Ricky
by Carol Koff
10″ × 8″, 2014

I love Jennifer's idea of combining photography and quilting. I have an abundance of photographs that I have taken over the years, and many of them were taken with the intention of using them in some way for art quilts. Now that I have taken Jennifer's workshop, I am able to use her technique to turn my photographs into art quilts. I think Ricky is very photogenic, and I have had this photograph for several years. I thought he would be a perfect subject for Jennifer's Thread Stories technique.

My Kids
by Iris Sonnenshein
20″ × 26″, 2014

This quilt was started in Jennifer's workshop in Santa Fe and finished at home. It's a photo I took of my children when they went out to play during a wet Maine vacation. I had expected their faces to require a long list of skin-tone colors, but I was amazed to find out how many colors were required to create the ponchos. Who knew there were so many variations on yellow and orange? I finished the quilt with metallic-thread swirls to suggest raindrops in the background and added the children's names to fill the larger empty space at the top left of the quilt.

Photo by Eugene Wong

!Gubi
by Susan Parzybok
20″ × 25″, 2014

This is the face of !Gubi, a San (Bushman) patriarch, living with his extended family in eastern Namibia near the Botswana border. The nomadic way of life is slowing disappearing for the Bushmen. This man and his family live in a small village, which we would describe as primitive, on a sheep farm owned by a local Afrikaans family. Their endangered language is San and has the characteristic click consonants. !Gubi holds the very root of civilization in the form of some of the oldest DNA found on earth. He also possesses some of the truly beautiful traits of men and women—a spirit full of kindness, joy, and love.

The Best Things in Life Are Free
by Linda Mullins Spirio; 20″ × 26″, 2014; based on an original photo by Jennifer Day

This little girl is fishing on the coast of Nicaragua. Most villagers live a subsistence life, and she is trying to reap the free bounty that is in the ocean. She's taken the hair bands out of her hair, and the sea breeze is blowing through her wavy locks. After spending many years as a mostly traditional quilter, I found thread painting this girl to be a freeing experience. That feeling, coupled with the girl's free-flowing hair and the joy of her pursuit, are the inspiration for the title of this artwork, which has a special place in my heart.

Savitri Temple Worshippers
by Gayle Ceppero; 24″ × 20″, 2014; based on an original photo by Morgan Ceppero

I feel very fortunate to have stumbled onto Jennifer's class in Santa Fe, New Mexico. Her technique is wonderful, and although I've done a fair amount of machine quilting I never thought about the option of actually painting with thread using her "shading" technique. Her mantra was "If it doesn't look the way you think it should, put another color on top." For example, in this quilt, I was not happy with the nose on the man with the dark blue turban. His nose looks different now than when this photograph was taken, thanks to a little more thread!

Tawny's Ready to Roll
by Jan Potter
20″ × 25″, 2014

Tawny's favorite activity was our daily walk each morning. She bounced all over as I said "walk" or even spelled it. As she aged, she had trouble keeping up with me, so I got the stroller she is sitting in. As you can see from the expression on her face, she loved it, and she got lots of attention from other walkers as they passed by. This was my first quilt using the Thread Stories technique.

Esmeralda
by Jan Holzbauer; 20″ × 23″, 2014; based on an orignal photo by Jennifer Day

I created this portrait based on one of Jennifer's photographs. I wanted to create an art quilt based on this photograph of Esmeralda because I love the character in her face and her sweet smile. I began work on the quilt in Jennifer's five-day workshop. My challenge was to learn to control the amount of thread that I used in her technique of thread painting. By using less thread, I was able to let the background fabric to do some of the work—allowing it to show through between the threads to create a seamlessly blended portrait.

A Prince among Kings
by Lois Poldony
27″ × 19″, 2014

After taking a fabulous five-day class with Jennifer and completing the piece I had begun in class, I created this quilt as my first solo attempt at thread painting. This artwork is based on a photograph I took of our two-year-old Cavalier King Charles spaniel, Flash. Normally the quilts I make take approximately two years to complete. This one, stitched with 52 different 30-weight polyester threads, was finished in less than two months! It was truly a joy to make something I was so proud of in such a short period of time.

Amelia Braving the North Shore
by Lois Poldony; 29″ × 19″, 2014; based on an original photo by Gary Poldony

My husband, Gary, took the photograph of our granddaughter upon which this quilt is based. Having learned to thread paint from Jennifer, I thought this seemed like the perfect opportunity to capture that day in thread. This is my third thread-painted quilt. I completed the thread painting of Amelia and the major rock formations in 47 different 30-weight polyester threads. Using 6 different variegated King Tut threads, I free-motion quilted, with numerous pebble variations, each color section.

This quilt made a wonderful gift for our son and daughter-in-law as a memento of our special day.

JENNIFER DAY portrait quilts

Abuela
by Jennifer Day
41″ × 48″, 2010

This is a quilt of an older Hispanic woman sitting in an open window of an old adobe home. Her demeanor is contemplative as she looks outside the window. My husband, Jimmy, and I are New Mexico ranchers. Our ranches are fairly remote and there are ruins of old buildings dating back to the early 1800s scattered throughout our ranches. This adobe building is an old church constructed in the early 1800s and abandoned in the early 1900s. Living in this remote portion of New Mexico is not easy, but with family near, life is good.

Cuban Guitar
by Jennifer Day
35″ × 27″, 2012

I took the photograph of these musicians as they played their music on Cathedral Plaza in Havana, Cuba. They come every day to the plaza to play their music for free for all to hear. They clearly love what they are doing. The twinkle in the old man's eye as he plays his guitar is priceless.

Dream Music
by Jennifer Day
39″ × 40″, 2011

This quilt is of a girl playing her violin in a totally white sanctuary. I caught the image of her in motion as she played. My goal in this quilt was to portray her movement. I chose to thread paint her body in its entirety. There are over 4200 yards of thread in her figure. That is more than two miles of thread. I quilted the background in a shadow detail. This detail is not regular in stitch length or width of line as to exemplify the motion of this young woman. The young woman played her violin for over an hour. Her hair escaped from her ponytail as she moved about the sanctuary. Her eyes were closed as she dreamed her music.

Boy and His Best Friend
by Jennifer Day
34″ × 34″, 2013

Boy and His Best Friend is a quilt featuring my 10-year-old son and his Old English sheepdog, B Bear. They definitely are best friends who spend hours together every day. The challenge of the quilt was capturing the love between the two of them in thread. The background is free-motion embroidery with less than ¼″ between lines of stitching.

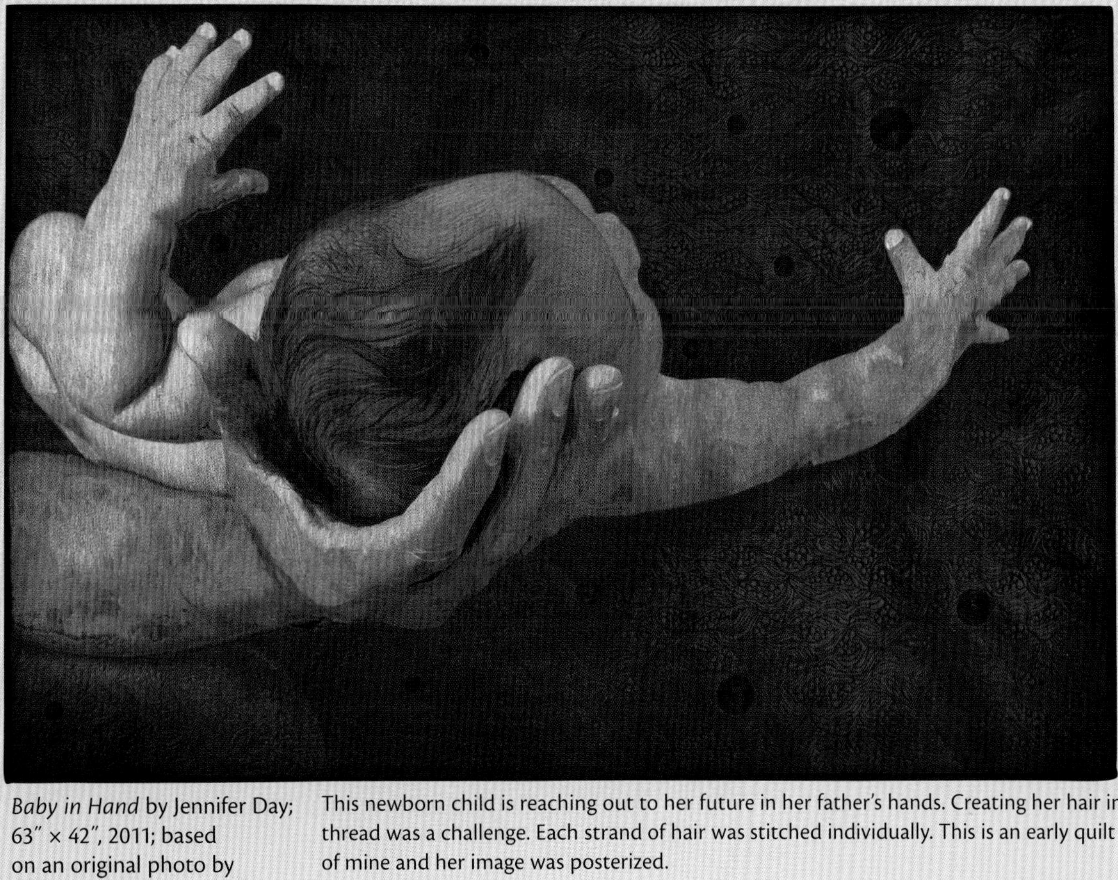

Baby in Hand by Jennifer Day; 63″ × 42″, 2011; based on an original photo by Barbara Helgason

This newborn child is reaching out to her future in her father's hands. Creating her hair in thread was a challenge. Each strand of hair was stitched individually. This is an early quilt of mine and her image was posterized.

Hot Day, Cool Water
by Jennifer Day
30″ × 41″, 2012

This quilt is based on a photograph of a young boy drinking water from a mountain stream in Colorado on a hot summer day. As this is an early quilt, I used the posterization process. I am sure his fingernails are clean because he was playing in the water!

When I Was Young
by Jennifer Day
34″ × 55″, 2012

As I roamed the streets of Havana with my camera, I found myself invited into this old woman's home. I turned from my conversation with her son and saw her sitting on the red naugahyde sofa in front of a peeling plaster wall and under a water-stained painting of a young woman inviting viewers to sample her wares. I could not resist snapping the photo. Upon reflection, this may have been the woman when she was young, taken in the 1950s. A family portrait?

Holy Cow
by Jennifer Day
43″ × 56″, 2011

"Gee … holy cow!" That is what my son and his best friend said as they wandered into a pasture of steers one day at our ranch in New Mexico. Once they realized where they were, they held on to each other in awe and trepidation. Then the steers began to move toward them. The next thing I knew the boys were running as fast as they could away from the animals! Ranch life was good that day.

Tibetan Treasure by Jennifer Day; 36″ × 28″, 2013; based on an original photo by Braden Gunem

This art quilt is based on a photograph of a Buddhist monk holding a cup of tea. The script is Tibetan mantras speaking of compassion, health, wisdom, and love. The dirt under the nails of the monk tells another story. Is he traveling in a third-world country where there is no running water? Stories!

Cooking with the Sun by Jennifer Day; 72″ × 72″, 2014; based on an original photo by Barbara Grover

Solar cooking is the simplest, safest, most convenient way to cook food without consuming fuel or heating up the kitchen. Many people choose to solar cook for these reasons. But for hundreds of millions of people around the world who cook over fires fueled by wood or dung, and who walk for miles to collect wood or spend much of their meager incomes on fuel, solar cooking is more than a choice—it is a blessing. For millions of people who lack access to safe drinking water and become sick or die each year from preventable waterborne diseases, solar water pasteurization is a lifesaving skill. There are numerous reasons to cook the natural way—with the sun.

Mmm ... Good
by Jennifer Day
22″ × 27″, 2013

Mmm ... Good is a quilt based on a photograph that I took of a two-year-old girl in a shopping cart at a grocery store. She really is enjoying this banana. Her puffy cheeks are full of her last bite. Her huge eyes, banana-touched lips, and hair create the perfect definition of mmm ... good. My guess is that she had become a bit cranky and her grandmother was desperate to finish her shopping without a crying child in her basket. A ripe banana was just the ticket. My guess is that she was a perfect child for the rest of the day!

Garden Wonder
by Jennifer Day
40″ × 36″, 2014

This is a quilt of a young boy carefully holding a butterfly. He had been happily playing in the dirt in the garden, digging up worms, when the butterfly came to rest in his hands. The butterfly stayed with him for quite a while as they shared the joy of a beautiful day outside on a warm summer day.

Tengo Hambre (I Am Hungry)
by Jennifer Day
42" × 50", 2014

These children live in an inhabited dump, Chinendega, in Nicaragua. I ventured into the dump just as the sister was bringing her brother a bowl of fish stew that my ten-year-old son and I had prepared for the children. The young boy had begun gathering treasures from the trash at dawn, uncovering them with his pickax. His pink bag is full of metal and plastics. By lunchtime, he was very dirty and tired. The bowl of soup was a welcome surprise. It is my honor to be able to chronicle these children's daily struggles and to share their story.

Carson and the Barn Cat
by Jennifer Day
20″ × 20″, 2014

Carson and the barn cat were outside, sitting on a fence one cool morning at the ranch in New Mexico, when I snapped this photograph. The cat was feral once upon a time, living in the barn and subsisting on rats and lizards. Hence his name—Killer. His origin is unknown, but he seems to have a bit of bobcat in his ancestry. Eventually, the cat lost his fear of humans and he and my son became fast friends, spending hours together on the ranch.

Cuban Ballerina
by Jennifer Day
38″ × 36″, 2015

This quilt is based on a photograph I took of a young woman who dances with the National Cuban Ballet. She was dancing in a grand old building that has become dilapidated with time and lack of resources in Havana. Her toe pointing at the base of the statue at the foot of the marble staircase draws attention to the combination of beauty and decay.

Judy
by Jennifer Day
40″ × 41″, 2015

I met Judy one day in the checkout line at a grocery store. She is the epitome of a woman balancing her work and personal life. Is she working because she enjoys people or because the state of her finances does not meet her needs? Perhaps both? I was immediately drawn to the stories that her countenance tells. Her wrinkles are many, but are also graceful and exhibit her fabulous personality. When she smiles, her face lights up with laugh lines.

about the author

Jennifer is an ASID-accredited interior designer, goldsmith, photographer, and art quilter who began quilting in 2010. Her photographs tell stories as they are covered in thread in her art quilts, depicting people in a realistic manner. Her unique technique, using up to 300 different colors of thread in a single quilt, has attracted interest from international galleries, museums, and publications.

Jennifer enjoys teaching her students how to tell stories in thread and enjoys giving lectures and workshops to guilds and groups. She has worked with Gütermann to develop the Jennifer Day Thread Stories line of threads, which offers 144 colors specifically chosen from the Mara line for thread-painted portraiture.

When not quilting, Jennifer is a rancher in New Mexico and travels to hospital and cancer wards with her Old English sheepdog, B Bear. She is married to Jimmy and has three children, the last of whom was a blessing when he unexpectedly arrived in this world when she was 48 years old.

People are my passion.
There is a story in everyone.
My goal is to help individuals
tell their stories through art.

~ Jennifer Day

resources

THREAD

Bergen Tailors & Cleaners Supply Corp.
bergentailorsupply.com

Isacord Thread
isacordthread.com

Presencia America
presenciaamerica.com

Superior Threads
superiorthreads.com

Thread Stories
jdaydesign.com

WAWAK Sewing
Gütermann threads and other sewing supplies
WAWAK.com

SEWING MACHINES

Brother
brother-usa.com/sewing

Handi Quilter
handiquilter.com

CANVAS

Big Duck Canvas Warehouse
bigduckcanvas.com

PAPER-BACKED FABRIC

Jacquard InkJet Fabric Systems
inkjetfabrics.com

Dharma Trading Co.
dharmatrading.com

Electric Quilt Company
electricquilt.com

SCISSORS

Handi Quilter
handiquilter.com

WAWAK Sewing
WAWAK.com

LIGHTING

Koncept Lighting
jdaydesign.com

FREE-MOTION QUILTING BOOKS

- Books by Leah Day
leahday.com
- *Shape by Shape Free-Motion Quilting* by Angela Walters
- *Modern Quilting Designs* by Bethany Peas
- *Doodle Quilting* by Cheryl Malkowski